NOV   '03

VILLAGE OF THE SMALL HOUSES

VILLAGE OF THE

IAN FERGUSON

SMALL HOUSES

A MEMOIR *of Sorts*

DOUGLAS & MCINTYRE
VANCOUVER / TORONTO

Douglas & McIntyre Ltd.
2323 Quebec Street, Suite 201
Vancouver, British Columbia
Canada V5T 4S7
www.douglas-mcintyre.com

National Library of Canada Cataloguing in Publication Data
Ferguson, Ian, 1959–
Village of the small houses : a memoir of sorts / Ian Ferguson.

ISBN 1-55365-021-2

1. Ferguson, Ian, 1959– —Childhood and youth.
2. Fort Vermilion (Alta.)—Biography. I. Title.
FC4199.F69Z49 2003   971.23'1   C2003-905382-2

Editing by Barbara Pulling
Jacket and text design by Jessica Sullivan
Front jacket photograph courtesy of Ian Ferguson
Printed and bound in Canada by Friesens
Printed on acid-free paper

We gratefully acknowledge the financial support
of the Canada Council for the Arts, the British Columbia Arts Council,
and the Government of Canada through the Book Publishing Industry
Development Program (BPIDP) for our publishing activities.

Permission to reprint excerpts from the song lyrics of
"I'm Moving On" by Hank Snow and "I've Been Everywhere" by Geoff Mack
and John Grenell granted by Warner/Chappell Music.
All rights reserved.

For Lorna Bell

contents

Village of the Small Houses is a memoir of sorts, or sort of a memoir. Take your pick. I was born and raised in Fort Vermilion, which is famous for two things. It set a record in 1911 for the lowest recorded temperature in Canada at sixty-one below, a record that wasn't beaten until 1947 by Snag, Yukon. And it was, at the time, the third-poorest community in Canada. Things have improved. Fort Vermilion is now the fifth-poorest community in the country.

This book is as honest as I could make it, but I haven't let the facts get in the way of the story I was trying to tell. Nothing that follows is true, except for the parts that really happened.

VILLAGE OF THE SMALL HOUSES

*B*IG
RIVER

Here's a word that you don't know. *Wayheoh*. It means, literally translated, "a long time away." Indian word. Bush Cree. It neatly combines "a long time ago" and "a place far away," but it has more significance than that. The thinking behind the word refers to a long distance travelled, both physically and chronologically, and what such a journey does to the person travelling. It's a good word. Great word. It's where we're going to start. A faraway place and a long-ago time. *Wayheoh*.

We're in the North. Not the Arctic, but as far north as you can get in Alberta before you bump into the territorial boundary. The True North. Up there. The middle of nowhere. It is snowing and it is cold and there isn't a whole lot to see. There are trees, scrub pine mainly, and there is a narrow road that twists and turns as it cuts through the forest, a rough stretch of dirt that, at the best of times, isn't in good condition. Right now, with the snow coming down and the wind blowing and the ice forming, this road is in the worst shape it ever gets. This is a road that a seismic crew chopped out of the woods sometime back in the 1930s, and no one has bothered with the upkeep on it since then. If you were driving it, you'd want to be behind the wheel of a big transport truck or an all-terrain vehicle. Maybe a tank. And even then you would creep along and drive as carefully as you could, because this road doesn't want you on it. Not at all. It is a succession of ugly deep ruts and even uglier and deeper potholes, and every now and then this road tosses up a patch of black ice in an attempt to throw you off its back and into the trees that are lined up on either side. The sun is going down, and the trees are tossing shadows across the road. At any moment you could veer into those trees, end up wrapped around them, tangled in their branches, and you'd want to die in the crash because the alternative would be to slowly freeze to death. It's that cold out.

Believe it or not, there is an automobile on this road. It is not a tank or a truck of any kind. It is a 1953 four-door two-toned green-and-white Mercury Zephyr, and it isn't creeping along, either. Despite the conditions, this car is flying, fishtailing out of curves and bottoming out on the rough patches, and the wheels are spitting up rocks and gravel and frozen chunks of mud, and the light from the headlights is stretching out through the darkness and dancing off the trees. The car is barely staying on the road.

That's my father behind the wheel. It's loud inside the car. The windshield wipers are snapping back and forth, thudding out a contrapuntal rhythm to the beating of his heart and the pounding in his head and the harsh, convulsive, gulping breaths he is taking. He has a cigarette clenched between his teeth—he hasn't fired it up, he hasn't had the time—and right now it is everything he can do to keep from careening into the trees. My father is no longer driving the car; not really. He's just sort of aiming it, and if he thought for one second about how close he is to the edge, he'd have to stop the car in the middle of the road and throw up.

That's my mother lying on the back seat. The rear window on one side is open a crack, and the wind is whistling through. It sounds like a teakettle on the boil, one continuous note that is awfully close to harmonizing with her long hissing breaths. She's not enjoying the ride. She is being bounced and tossed around, and she would dearly love to tell my father to slow down and take it easy, except she can't seem to get the words out. She's a shade over eight months pregnant, she's in a world of pain, and she is so ready to have the baby that she thinks maybe slowing down wouldn't be such a good idea after all. Even so, if she could manage to sit up and look out, if she could really see how my father is driving, she'd probably tell him to stop the car in the middle of the road and let her out.

The car is the first automobile my father ever bought brand-new. Cash deal, and it was once his pride and joy. He used to baby that car, but even though it's only six years old, you can already tell it has seen better days. There has been some heavy wear and tear on that vehicle. Mileage. Serious mileage. It's a small sedan, or at least small for the style of the day, but my mother is still able to lie down flat in the back seat. The only thing she can think of doing to keep herself in one position is pressing her feet against the rear door as hard as she can. It isn't making much of a difference, but it does take her mind off her situation for a second or two, and, oh my Lord, why does it have to hurt so much? She makes a noise, and it sounds bad, really bad, but she can't help herself.

"Hold on, Louise, we're almost there."

That's my father speaking. He is trying to reassure my mother, but his jaw is so tight, with the cigarette still clenched between his teeth, that his voice comes out in a high-pitched squeak that is not the least bit reassuring, no sir. If he wanted to calm my mother down, well, he hasn't managed that. Plus, he sprays tobacco from his unlit cigarette all over the windshield.

The baby my mother is expecting is me. It is early in November, and I am not supposed to arrive for another two or three weeks. But it doesn't matter what the calendar says, let alone what some doctor has figured out as far as a due date goes, I'm on my way right now. I'm in a hurry, and so are my parents. Not only because I'm showing up unfashionably early, but also because they are trying to catch the last ferry across the river. This isn't the last ferry for the day, which would be bad enough; this is the last ferry going across for at least six months, maybe as much as nine. It depends on what kind of winter is in store.

The Fort Vermilion ferryboat landing sits where the mighty Peace River bends and turns to the north, before heading back down south again. The landing is also known as The Narrows, because the Peace River is only half a mile wide at this spot. That's why they put the ferry crossing there. The river is well over a mile across at the widest sections, and it is fast. This river moves. It doesn't matter how quickly it goes, however, because this is the time of year when the cold beats it. The temperature drops and ice begins to form, and at a certain point the river is simply impassable. The ferry is pulled out of service, and everybody waits for the river to freeze solid. It takes at least three weeks for the river to ice up, maybe as much as six; depends on how cold it gets. If I'd waited long enough, the ice bridge would have been ready and my parents could have driven to the hospital right across the top of the river. That was the original plan.

Well, hell, men make plans, and God laughs. That's the big joke. When you've got your fingers crossed and you're hoping things will somehow come together and work out for you, that's when you're into the land of "if." My father was in that land now, and it wasn't any comfort to him. There were a lot of "ifs." If he could keep the car on the road and if the ferry was still running and if they could get across the river fast enough and if he could get to the hospital on time and if my premature emergence into the world wasn't a sign of more serious problems . . . if everything fell into place, well, things might just turn out okay. If. If. If.

The road makes one final bend, one last attempt to send my parents into the ditch, and then it heads straight downhill towards the river. They've made it. They are at the crossing, and nobody could say they didn't do it in record time. And there is the ferry, sitting on the shore waiting for them. So far, so good. That's what my father is thinking now, and he keeps repeating it to himself. "So far, so good." He doesn't realize that he's saying it out loud. He thinks he's keeping it to himself, but my mother can hear him saying something. She can't make out the words, and this is adding to her anxiety.

"Hank," my mother says—and that's what she calls him, even though his full and proper name is Henry—"will you please be quiet?"

My father doesn't answer. He's busy snaking the car onto the other side of the road; that would be the oncoming lane, if anyone was getting off the ferry, or if the road was well enough designed to have lanes in the first place. He also knows that whenever my mother is really mad at him, she calls him by his full and proper name. Since she hasn't done that, he doesn't feel he has to pay attention. He has a plan. He's planning to jump the queue and go to the front of the line, and his hope is that the operator will let him onto the ferry and then push off, leaving everybody else waiting for the next trip across, if there is one. That's his plan. Since it involves cutting in front of people who are patiently waiting their turn to board, the plan's success revolves around whoever has drawn the duty of driving the ferryboat on the last day of the season.

Since this will be the last ferry run until spring, most people in the area have already laid in supplies and prepared themselves to hunker down until the ice solids up. Everybody knows better than to wait until the last minute. You wouldn't want to end up stranded on the wrong side of the river. So there are only a handful of people waiting to board the ferryboat. There are a couple of dusty pickups, one battered station wagon and one real wagon being pulled by a team of horses. All the vehicles are full of provisions, including the real wagon, which is also full to the brim with Mennonites.

There's not a lot of room to manoeuvre, but he manages. He skids to a halt right at the end of the landing and jumps out of the car. He is thrilled to see that the fellow in charge of the ferry that evening isn't "that prick Joe Beck," as my father always refers to the manager of the Fort Vermilion and District ferry service. It is Bud Peyen, which is a huge break for my father. Bud Peyen is driving the ferry. Bud Peyen is my father's faithful Indian companion, his loyal sidekick. What they are, racial differences notwithstanding, is friends.

Bud Peyen is also the only person in the entire North who can look down on my father. Literally. Bud stands six feet, eight inches high, which makes him three inches taller than my dad. They are both big men, but that's where the similarities end. Bud Peyen is broad across the chest and solid throughout. My father is so lean that Bud Peyen used to say he'd have to run around in a rainstorm to get wet. Forty years later, they'll look completely different. Bud Peyen will end up nothing but skin and bones, and my father will be all swollen up. They'll look opposite to how they look now. But this won't happen until just before they die, and neither of them has given much thought to what he is going to look like at the end of his life, let alone when it is going to finish up. At this point in time, they've both got other things to worry about.

My father is worried about my mother. And me, I suppose, although we haven't met as of yet. Bud Peyen is worried that my father is going to crash his car into one of the pickup trucks or ram the station wagon that has already loaded. He's also concerned that my father has gone crazy, since he is out of the car almost before it stops and he's running, actually running, slipping and sliding and almost falling, and nothing that's coming out of his mouth is explaining the situation.

"Bud, we've got to leave, we've got to go, let's get moving, let's go, let's go, let's go, right now, right now . . . "

My father keeps talking that way, in one continuous sentence, not making a lick of sense, which is a little unnerving for Bud Peyen. My father is still speaking in that high-pitched squeaky voice, which is disturbing in itself. His eyes are wild, and his whole manner makes it look as if he's gone off the deep end. He might even be dangerous. Bud Peyen would normally just knock a crazy person cold, drop him in his tracks, but this is my father. He is teaching Bud Peyen to read and write, and Bud considers my father to be the smartest man he's ever met, even if he's not actively demonstrating that intelligence right now.

Bud spots my mother in the back seat. She is struggling to sit up, and Bud holds up one enormous hand to get my father to stop speaking. Then he ambles over to the car to see if maybe my mother can explain things. This is taking longer than my father would like. He is right behind Bud, and although he'd love to continue to talk and talk and talk, he's managing to restrain himself. But he's breathing so heavily it sounds as if he's going to have a massive heart attack. Or maybe a stroke. Either way, it's a concern, and it's making Bud Peyen tense. He leans over to chat to my mother, bending himself nearly in half. He's hoping she'll say something that will make it easy for him to excuse my father's rude behaviour.

"Louise?"—and this is Bud Peyen now—"What's the . . . oh my good God!"

Bud takes one look at the condition my mother is in, and he gets the message. Not from how pregnant she is; she's too bundled up for him to notice that. But from the look on her face, which is soaked in sweat and tears, and, quite frankly, from the noise she is making as she tries to sit up and tell him what's going on. It's the same noise she made in the car earlier, only worse, and it chills Bud Peyen through to the middle. Bud may be a big man, but he can move fast when he needs to, and he leaps into action. He swings open the door on the driver's side, picks my father up by the scruff of his neck and throws him into the car. This takes the wind out of my father, and he is forced to waste valuable time looking for his glasses, which have flown off and fallen to the floor. He doesn't lose hold of his cigarette, but it does crimp up a little. Bud kicks the car door shut with a gigantic boot, then races down to the ferry. The drivers and passengers of the other vehicles have started to get out to see what's taking so long. Except for the Mennonites in the wagon; they're a patient people, and able to overcome any natural curiosity they might have. Actually, everybody is behaving very graciously. There's some grumbling and muttering, but nobody is planning to get into an argument with Bud Peyen. Besides, Bud's yelling something at them. Since he's known to be a fellow of few words, everybody listens up to hear what he has to say.

"We've got an emergency." This seems straightforward to everyone on the shore, and there is nodding and shrugging from the people who have lost their place in line. Sure. Has to be something important. Why else would Bud Peyen move that fast?

"It's the schoolteacher and his wife." Sure. That tall fellow from out, that's who that is. Can't say I've ever met his wife, though.

"She's got to get to the hospital right now." This sends everybody back into their vehicles, which pleases Bud Peyen no end.

He's already waving my father onto the ferry. It takes finesse on my father's part, since he has to get the Zephyr in on an angle to avoid the first pickup truck, and the loading platform is bucking and swaying. The moment the back bumper clears the lip of the ferry, Bud slams the safety gate closed and heads for the wheelhouse. Before he disappears into the cabin, he thinks to call out the rest of the explanation.

"She's having a baby." This seems satisfactory to everybody waiting, especially when Bud adds "right now." The Mennonites aren't too impressed; they have huge families, and giving birth isn't that big a deal. But they are a polite people, so they don't put up a fuss. The last thing Bud Peyen yells before the belch of the diesel engine drowns him out is "Don't worry, we'll come back for you."

What nobody knows is that Bud Peyen, a man renowned for his honesty and character, has just told three big lies. Not that any of them is his fault. The first lie was referring to my father as "the schoolteacher." True, my father is employed as a grade school teacher at the Indian school in Fort Vermilion, but he is not, if you want to get specific about it, either qualified or licensed to be a teacher by profession.

That's the first big lie. Of course, Bud Peyen has no way of knowing this at the time. The second big lie was when he referred to my mother as my father's wife. This is not technically true, either. Although my father and mother live together, and are about to have their second baby, they are not actually married. Well. Not in the legal or religious sense, at any rate. Still, this isn't anything Bud Peyen could possibly know, since my parents go to a fair bit of effort not to let on that they are "living in sin."

The third big lie was the one that will most directly affect everybody waiting for the ferry. And it's the only one they might have worried seriously about, had they known they were being lied to. Some of them might have been a little concerned about my father and his almost complete lack of qualifications, but most of them couldn't have cared less that my parents weren't truly husband and wife. Despite the moral climate of the late 1950s, this part of the world has a slightly more flexible view of marriage. This is, after all, the North.

The third and biggest lie was when Bud Peyen told them he'd come back for them. The truth of the matter is that every single person waiting on the banks of the Peace River is going to have to make other arrangements. Again, this wasn't a deliberate lie on Bud Peyen's part; he simply has no way of knowing that the ferry isn't coming back. Ever.

The Fort Vermilion and District ferry is a paddlewheel boat. Not like the ones they have way down south. This is a flatbed, a plain metal frame with wood beams laid across to make the deck and a plywood shack built out over the side to keep the operator warm. If you're standing in the wheelhouse, you can look directly down at the paddlewheel itself. It is a cast-iron contraption about six feet in diameter that resembles a fat bicycle tire, only with wood slats attached to the spokes to catch the water. A persnickety old diesel motor that was removed from a combine harvester powers the operation, and the ferry runs on a metal cable that was stretched across the river during the Second World War by members of the Canadian Corps of Engineers. This had something to do with wartime security, but it was a great benefit to everybody in the area. Prior to construction, the only way across the river was by boat in summer, when the current wasn't too strong. Other than that, you could walk over when winter hit. There is a story that one of the soldiers involved in running the cable fell into the river and drowned, but that could just be a legend. There's not much to driving the damn thing. All Bud Peyen has to do to get the ferry moving is to start the engine and put it in first gear.

There isn't any steering involved, the cable takes care of that, and the only trick is remembering to turn off the engine at the right moment so that you don't come up too hard and crash into the opposite shore. Bud Peyen has been running the ferry for over three years, and he is proudly crash-free. In fact, he has a reputation as the best ferryboat operator working. He can glide that ferry into a landing so gently you don't know you've stopped.

My father isn't convinced they've started. He heard the motor turn over, and the paddlewheel start splashing, but the ferry doesn't seem to be moving. He gets out of the car to make sure they are well and truly under way, and it is only when he can see the shore slipping away into the darkness that he relaxes enough to finally light his cigarette. By this point, it has lost so much tobacco that it flashes up and goes out. It is like a shooting star, or a tiny flare. So bright and so fast that it blinds him for a second. He is blinking the spots out of his eyes and fumbling for the car door when he notices that someone is getting out of the only other vehicle on the ferry. He can barely make out the shape of the person, but the voice is unmistakable.

"Bud, what the hell are you doing?"

It is, of course, that prick Joe Beck, now waddling over to the wheelhouse. My father can tell not only by his voice but by his silhouette in the night. Joe Beck is a short, perfectly round man who is forever running out of breath. If you were to draw him, you'd take a piece of paper and make three circles, one on top of the other. If my father hadn't been so distracted, he would have recognized that prick Joe Beck's station wagon as being the only other vehicle that had made it on board.

"You can't take off without a full load." It is obvious that Joe Beck is not too happy about what is going on. He isn't exactly shouting, but you can easily hear his wheezing whine over the clunking of the diesel engine. He might be angry, but he also has a point; fully loaded, the ferry can take six cars or four trucks or two hay wagons or any combination of the above. One station wagon and one sedan isn't anywhere near a proper trip.

Bud Peyen comes out on the deck and tries to think of something to say that will calm things down. The problem is that Bud becomes a little tongue-tied around white people, having grown up with the idea that they are in charge of the world, and here he is trying to explain himself to the supervisor of the Fort Vermilion and District ferry service, who is not only white but also Bud's boss. The only white person Bud isn't nervous around is my father, which may be why they became friends. My father might not have known that that prick Joe Beck was on board, but Bud Peyen certainly did, and he still broke the rules to help out his friend. It isn't the first time his friendship with my father is going to get him in trouble.

"Now, Bud, goddamnit, you've got to turn this boat around." He doesn't actually mean that the ferry should make a circle; even Joe Beck isn't that stupid. What he means is that Bud Peyen should turn off the motor, put it into reverse gear, and head back in the direction they've come from.

"Well." This is all Bud Peyen says.

"Bud, goddamnit, this is the last run. We're not going to leave those folks stranded."

"Hmm." Bud is having the same problem he has whenever someone is mad at him. He can think of what to say, it's there in his head, but it somehow seems to get stuck in his throat.

"That's it, I'm telling you, that's it! I will go and turn the goddamn thing around myself." This is when my father decides to get involved, the idea of turning the ferry around not fitting into his plans. He steps in between Bud Peyen and that prick Joe Beck.

"Listen," my father says, "you shouldn't be angry at Bud—" He is prepared to go into a perfectly good explanation of why, but he never gets the chance.

"Goddamnit, Hank," says Joe Beck, "this is none of your god-damn business! You go back and sit in your car." To emphasize his seriousness and his anger, Joe Beck stabs my father in the chest with a pointed finger. My father is not a fighter, he is more of a talker, but he's at the end of his rope, and enough is enough. He grabs that prick Joe Beck by the arm, his fingers sinking into the doughy flesh. He lifts him off the deck and half drags/half carries him over to the Zephyr. Bud Peyen can't believe his eyes. He's never thought of my father as being a man of action. But there you go. My father throws the little man against the side of the car, then leans over until their faces almost touch.

"Joe," my father says, in a tone so even and reasonable that it is terrifying, "have you ever delivered a baby?"

"What? Goddamnit, no, of course not."

"Well," says my father, "you're going to have to, because my wife is about to give birth right here and right now, if you don't keep this ferryboat moving." For emphasis, he twists the little man around so that he can see my mother in the back seat, adding, to drive the point home, "You little prick."

My mother looks up and sees my father holding that prick Joe Beck by the neck, pressing his frightened face up against the window. This strikes her as humorous. She starts to laugh, but she can't quite manage it. The pain hits her again. Her body jack-knifes, and she makes another one of those noises.

He may be a prick, but even Joe Beck is able to figure out what's going on. He breaks free of my father and races over to Bud Peyen. "Bud, goddamnit, put this sonovabitch into high gear, the schoolteacher's wife is going to have a baby!"

"That's what I was trying to tell you."

Bud is in the wheelhouse so fast it seems as if he vanished off the deck and reappeared inside the cabin. He is switching the gears so hard they're grinding, which makes him wince, but the goal is to get to top speed as quickly as possible. Nobody knows that engine better than Bud, and he is the best ferryboat operator there is, so he is pushing everything to the limit. The ferry, which has been chugging along sedately, lurches forward. The paddle-wheel starts slapping the water in double time, and it looks as if the ferry is going to set a record for making the opposite shore. Then the slats on the wheel start coming off.

The problem is, the ice has already started forming. Chunks of frozen river are making their way downstream, most of them still fairly small: eight or nine inches wide, five or six inches deep. Normally they wouldn't be dangerous, but at this speed they're bouncing against the paddlewheel, cracking the wood, and the momentum of the wheel is sending bits and pieces of wood flying through the air and into the water. It's strangely beautiful.

"Jee-zuz. Hank, we've gotta slow this sonovabitch down."

"Joe," says my father, "you do that and I'm going to have to hurt you." This may be a bluff, but that prick Joe Beck isn't taking any chances. He looks over at Bud Peyen, takes a second to catch his breath, then calls out in his loudest voice, "Never mind, Bud, let the sonovabitch rip."

So Bud Peyen lets it rip. He has a sad look on his face, and it might be because of the damage he's causing to the ferry, but it's as likely to be disappointment in that prick Joe Beck and his use of the term "sonovabitch." Bud has always thought of the ferry as a woman.

It's not so bad. A few pieces of wood broken off? Shouldn't be difficult to fix. That's what everyone on board the ferry is thinking, except my mother. She's thinking that my father should be in the car with her, not out on the deck gazing at who knows what. She doesn't know how fast the ferry is travelling or what sort of damage is happening. Even if she did, she wouldn't worry about it.

The piece of ice that kills the ferry has been floating down the Peace River for several days, bobbing in the current, making itself a little larger as the temperature drops, bumping occasionally into the shore, sticking there for a few hours, then continuing downstream. Eventually it will reach a width of three feet or so and a depth of close to five. At the lowest speed possible, the ferry can handle one or two larger pieces of ice; the bow usually nudges them away from the paddlewheel, or the ferryboat operator eases them out of the way with a metal pole kept expressly for that purpose. But get too many of these tiny icebergs in your path and you aren't going anywhere.

It is the sole responsibility of the manager of the Fort Vermilion and District ferry service to keep an eye on the river conditions and to announce when the last scheduled run will occur. Then, when spring break-up comes around, to decide when the river is clear enough to resume service. Most people feel Joe Beck closes the ferry down too soon in the fall and opens it too late in the spring. It is a generally held belief that he does this to save money, since the ferryboat operators, such as Bud Peyen, are seasonal and paid by the shift. Joe Beck is a government employee, paid year-round. From Joe Beck's perspective, the decision to shut down ferry service is made purely with safety in mind. Not that you can convince the locals this is true. He is dead right about the river conditions this time, though. The big chunk of ice misses the bow of the ferry and runs into the paddlewheel just as a slat clears the water. The speed of the boat wedges the chunk of ice firmly into the larger-than-normal gap created by a missing piece of wood, and the extra weight causes the paddlewheel to seize up. It is very dramatic. The paddlewheel lifts partway out of the water, high enough for Bud Peyen to identify the problem, then it stops turning. The diesel engine is working so hard to keep the flywheel moving that it starts to smoke. Bud is trying to dislodge the ice when he realizes the motor is in trouble.

"Joe," he says, "can you do me a favour?" Bud Peyen is still relentlessly polite. "Could you turn off the engine?"

Now, this is where it would be nice to report that my father does something to save the day, or at least to help out. He doesn't. He gets himself in the car and braces himself against the steering wheel. He does remember to spare a thought for my mother.

"Hold on, Louise, we might be coming in hard."

It is the worst landing Bud Peyen has ever made. The paddle-wheel is twisted and bent, and this has turned the ferry sideways, so that instead of drifting straight into the waiting dock the boat comes up over the edge. It is apparent that the motor should have been turned off earlier, because the ferry lands with, if not an actual crash, enough of a thump to shake everybody up. The boat is wedged high on the landing for a moment or two, and then it slowly grinds backwards, tearing off the few remaining slats on the paddlewheel, before shuddering to a halt. My father starts his car. He rolls down his window.

"Joe," he says, "could you stand up and get that gate dropped?"

The loading door is wrestled into position. My father bounces the Zephyr off the ferry and heads up the hill. Since the roadway on this side of the river is nicely gravelled, he stands on the accelerator. He's doing thirty miles an hour by the time he reaches the top of the hill, forty by the time he reaches the Fort Vermilion turnoff, and over fifty by the time he passes the Experimental Farm. He doesn't touch the brakes until he reaches the doors of St. Theresa's Catholic Hospital. He's out of the car and into the hospital, and he gets those nuns moving; they can tell he's serious, and they have my mother in the delivery room in no time flat. My father doesn't go in with her, that wasn't done in those days, but he's pleased to be there, he's going to make up for the fact that he was out of town when his first child was born, and . . . shit! *The first child.*

My father leaves the following message for my mother. He tells it to the duty nurse, who isn't a nun, but who is certainly Catholic in both religion and temperament. She repeats it verbatim to my mother as the doctor is examining her.

"'Tell Louise I forgot the baby clothes, so I've gone back for them.'"

The bag of hand-me-down baby clothes I am supposed to wear home from the hospital is, in fact, sitting in the trunk of the car. My father hasn't forgotten the baby clothes. He has, however, forgotten the baby.

My parents have been given free housing by the Peace River Separate School District as part of my father's employment. They live in what is called a teacherage, across the river from Fort Vermilion in a scattering of houses known as Rocky Lane. These aren't luxury accommodations. They are single-room cabins, without electricity or plumbing, heated by a wood stove, and not particularly well insulated, despite the climate of the area. They aren't built on a normal foundation, either. Since the ground freezes and buckles every year, each teacherage sits up on a frame of railway ties. To keep the floor warm in the winter, you have to surround the house with bales of hay and then bank snow up over that for insulation. There is an outhouse for use in the summer and a chemical toilet for indoor use when the weather gets too cold.

Neither of my parents was born in the North. My mother is not a delicate person by any means, but her eight months in Fort Vermilion have stretched her resilience as far as it can go. Living there in the year 1959 is like going back in time a hundred years. She doesn't find the accommodations to her liking, and she doesn't see the sense of living across the river and fifteen gruelling miles of dirt road away from the school where my father teaches. The public school board is building new housing, with electricity, for their teachers right in town. Those houses would make looking after my brother easier, since they'll also have running water. But they won't be finished until summer, and neither she nor my father has plans to stick around that long.

My father found the idea of the river freezing up confusing at first. If he lived on the other side of the river, he asked Gene Rogers, principal of both the Indian and the separate schools, how would he get to work in the winter?

"Well, Hank," Gene Rogers said, "you can bunk in with one of the teachers in town, or you can wait across the river for freeze-up to finish."

"With all due respect, Gene, if I wait across the river, I won't be doing any teaching."

"Hank," Gene Rogers said, and this was intended as a dismissal, "these are Indian kids. It doesn't matter if you teach them or not. They don't learn much."

Back at the Fort Vermilion ferryboat landing, Bud Peyen has just lost his job. Which is a blow, no doubt about it, but not nearly as shocking as seeing my father drive back down the hill. Bud is really surprised by that. He goes over to my father.

"Well, you were ever quick." Then he notices my mother is no longer in the car. "Hank, is everything okay?"

"Actually, Bud, no. I need to go back across the river."

"Hank, that's not going to happen. The ferry's shot. Paddle-wheel is busted up. Motor ain't working. Joe had to drive up to the RCMP, get them to radio across to the park ranger. He's going to drive down and tell those people we ain't coming back. Even if the ferry could take the trip, I wouldn't be driving it. I'm through."

"Well, you see, Bud, here's the problem. I left my son at my house . . . wait a second. He fired you?"

"You left your boy all alone?" They are each a step behind in the conversation, there being a lot to take in. "Yep, he fired me."

"That little prick," my father says. And then, almost as if to shift the blame, "Didn't you notice my son wasn't in the car?"

"You can't wreck the ferry and expect to keep your job," Bud says. Then, thoughtfully, "Yeah, I figured you had someone looking after him."

There is a long pause. Neither of them seems to want to say anything. Bud Peyen is thinking really, really hard.

"Jeez, Hank, how could you do that?"

"In the panic and confusion, I clean forgot him."

"How could you forget your own son?"

"I didn't do it on purpose."

"Didn't Louise notice you didn't bring him?"

"She should have; she was the one who got him dressed." My father was still trying to shift the blame. "She left him on the bed, before I put her in the car."

"That's terrible."

"That's why I have to get back across the river."

"Hank, it's impossible."

My father plays his ace. Bud Peyen has been coming over to the teacherage every Sunday for the past three weeks for dinner and reading lessons. He has already chewed his way through the alphabet.

"Bud, it's the same thing I said when you told me you didn't think you could ever learn to read or write." My father pauses to light up another cigarette, letting this sink in. "Nothing is impossible."

And that's how my father and Bud Peyen ended up taking a steel-bottomed rowboat across the Peace River during the fall ice formation. Twice. The boat comes courtesy of the Hudson's Bay store manager, and making the trip is foolish and dangerous and necessary. They cross at the foot of the old Factor's House, rowing with the current, and make good time. They don't talk much on the first crossing; they are both a bit concerned about my brother, Dan. It takes some doing once they land, but my father convinces Soorey Cardinal, who has been abandoned on the far shore, to drive them to the teacherage. Dan is still sleeping when they reach him, right where my mother left him, warm and comfortable, and they bundle him up and take him back down to the rowboat. The sun is starting to come up.

The trip back has one or two truly scary moments, when the ice comes out of nowhere and spins the boat, and my father has to stop rowing and grab my brother to make sure he stays in one place. Both men do a lot of talking. Mainly things like "This is easy," or "I'm not too tired," or "We're almost there." They are that frightened. My brother is only slightly over three years old, and sleepy. He doesn't say much at all.

On the way out, in the darkness, the entire town lined their vehicles up on the riverbank and shone their headlights for a beacon. Even that prick Joe Beck. They are still there waiting when my father and Bud Peyen step out of the rowboat with Dan. Nobody applauds or cheers, but everybody is happy they made it. It is mainly an Indian crowd, and they aren't much for cheering and clapping, though they do nod with appreciation for the risky adventure the two men have survived.

Bud Peyen and my father stop to catch their breath when they reach the top of the hill. Bud grins and shakes his head.

"Hank," he says, "you are probably the smartest person I've ever met, but what we just did?"

"Yes, Bud?"

"That was the stupidest thing ever."

I was born on either November 3 or November 4, depending who you want to believe. My mother gave birth a couple of hours after midnight on November 4, at almost exactly the time my father and Bud Peyen were starting across the river to pick up my brother. My father would always insist that I was born on the third, though, and that's what it says on my birth certificate. He's the one who did the paperwork. He was in the hospital on

November 3, so technically he was there for my birth. I guess that made sense to him somehow, some way. The argument continued long into my adulthood.

At the same time I was being born, give or take a few hours, Lloyd Loonskin was also coming into the world. He was born at home, in his grandmother's cabin. There was much less excitement surrounding his birth. He had been an easy pregnancy, even though his mother was only sixteen years old when she had him. Lloyd Loonskin's grandmother was the only other person around to welcome him. It's a good thing she was around. Three months later Lloyd Loonskin's mother walked out onto the frozen Peace River and laid herself down. She never got up again.

I was born lucky.

He was lucky to be born.

That made all the difference.

two

CLEAN GETAWAY

My parents ended up in the True North because of certain events that happened one day in March, in Edmonton, in the same year I was born. Nineteen fifty-nine.

On that particular day my mother was sitting in a rocking chair, gazing out a window. The city looked as if a dust storm had blown through, all concrete-grey and dirty. There hadn't been much snow that year, but what little had fallen was sticking close to the ground in muddy brown hedgehog-shaped piles. Not real snow. Not really spring yet, either. It wasn't that cold outside, but there was a chill in the air.

The window my mother was looking out belonged to a four-storey building right downtown. In the heart of the city, as they say. The building was named MacDougall Court. (Don't bother looking for it; they tore it down and paved it over years ago.) MacDougall Court rented out what used to be called cold-water flats. Single rooms, with a shared bathroom down the hall. No pets, no cooking, no liquor. No Indians Allowed.

Despite the exclusivity regarding their clientele, MacDougall Court was considered a less than desirable address. Besides having no elevator, most of the time it had no heat. Except in the summer; then it got plenty hot. Nice view, though. The building was perched on the side of a hill, right above the river valley. If you turned your head to the left and looked due north, you could watch the comings and goings at the MacDonald Hotel, which is what my mother was doing.

This was one of her favourite ways to pass the time. She'd hold my big brother, Dan, and rock back and forth and think about how nice it would be to stay in a place like the MacDonald Hotel. A place that had hot and cold running water, and elevators so that you didn't have to walk up four sets of stairs carrying a baby carriage and a baby to get to your room. A place that was so, well, so nice. The MacDonald was just about the finest hotel between Toronto and the Rocky Mountains. Still is. Sure, it went through a brief downturn during the 1970s, but they finally got rid of that godawful addition they slapped on the place, and the building has been restored and renovated. You could argue that there isn't a classier hotel in Alberta.

My mother was watching the hotel guests come and go, and making up stories about them for my brother. He was just a baby, really, so he had no opinion on the place. She imagined what the rooms were like, and what kind of people could afford to stay there, and what kind of food they served at the restaurant. My mother had never been inside the MacDonald. Once, while out with my brother for some air, she'd wandered over to take a gander at the lobby, but the doorman had come out to greet her, all dressed up in a dark red overcoat with brass buttons and a fur hat, looking as if Jesus Christ had joined the military, and she'd lost her nerve.

My mother was pregnant with me that March, and it was pretty much Dan's fault. He'd fooled her into wanting another baby. He was such a calm fellow, my brother. Thoughtful. Slept through the night. Hardly ever cried. He had been an easy pregnancy, and his birth was virtually pain-free. No morning sickness, no complications, no big deal. Have another kid? Easy. Except the kid on the way was me, and I was already causing my mother a whole world of problems. Most obviously, I was making her sick. Not just in the mornings, either, but morning, noon and night. She'd been desperate for some relief. On this particular day, however, she was enjoying her first non-nauseated afternoon in three weeks, courtesy of a kindly old doctor she'd gone to see at the free clinic.

My mother had walked over to the free clinic a few days earlier, carrying my brother. After a lengthy wait, the doctor said he had something that would fix her right up. It was a new drug, and not widely available in Canada, but he happened to have some samples. It was called thalidomide. My mother had taken her pills, and now she was feeling fine. It was a good day. That was the thought in her head: what a good day. Then my father came home.

My father didn't come into the room the way he usually did, with a smile and a joke and a promise about how prosperity was just around the corner. He liked to make my mother laugh, she had a terrific laugh, and he didn't like to see her worried. So he'd tell her about the sales he'd made or the funny people he had met. Once in a while he would suggest going out for Chinese food. My father must have thought Chinese food was the cure for worrying, because he and my mother were regular customers at Wing's Chinese and Canadian Café, which was west of the MacDonald Hotel on Jasper Avenue. (The café is still there, though some of the neon burned out a few years ago. You'll want to keep your eyes open for a sign that reads "Win Chin Ca Ca." And I wouldn't recommend dropping in for a meal; they stopped cleaning the place right after they lost my parents as customers. It's up to you, but I wouldn't eat there.)

So. The door at MacDougall Court opened, and in came my father, and this is what he did. He picked up the straight-backed chair that sat next to the bureau, turned it around, and wedged it under the door handle. Then he slid the bureau against the door as well. He didn't seem panicked, or nervous, or even in any kind of hurry. He seemed methodical. This might have been an attempt to keep my mother from getting worried, but it had the opposite effect.

"Hank," my mother said, "what's wrong?"

My father didn't answer; he just pulled out their suitcases from under the bed and started emptying clothes into them. He wasn't doing it quickly. He was taking things nice and easy. This made my mother more anxious.

"Hank?"

"Pack up the boy, Louise, we're leaving."

"Why are we leaving?"

"I can't go into that right now."

"Where are we going?"

"You know," my father said—and this time his nerves must have got to him, because he closed the first suitcase just a little too forcibly, causing my mother to jump just a little bit—"I don't really have a plan yet, but we have to leave. Right now."

My mother opened her mouth to say something, then changed her mind. My mother has never been anything but whip smart, and it didn't take her long to put everything in perspective. She didn't know what was going on, but she did know that someone or something was going to be at the door soon, and she didn't have any intention of sticking around to find out what they wanted. She ran around the room, frantically packing up her baby gear, not to mention her baby.

They exited through the window and started down the fire escape. It must have been a humorous sight, my father barely managing their three suitcases, my mother hanging on to my brother for dear life. Down the metal steps, onto the third-floor landing, and around the corner. Down the steps to the second-floor landing and around the corner. Down the steps to the first-floor landing, around the corner, down the steps . . . and when they had almost reached the bottom, it started raining.

The next phase of the operation was to reach the car. The 1953 green-and-white Mercury Zephyr. The car was a constant point of contention between them. As you may have figured out, they weren't living in the lap of luxury, and whenever money became an issue, my mother would bring up the car.

"We should sell the car," she'd say.

My father would sigh and shake his head. In as reasonable a tone as possible, he'd reply, "If we sell the car, we won't have any way of getting around."

"I bet we could get five hundred dollars for that car."

"But we wouldn't have any transportation." And on they went. Every couple has some never-ending argument playing on a loop as background music. The never-ending argument usually involves money, and occasionally a vehicle of some kind. So I don't want you to think that my parents were in the habit of arguing. They weren't. The arguments came later. At this stage of the game they were still getting along famously, even though they were about to take it on the lam.

They took a different route than usual to get to the garage where the car was parked, going through some alleys and across an empty lot. Once they'd climbed in, my father ran out of steam. He didn't start the engine. Instead, he sat there staring out the windshield. He had a strange look on his face, not as if he was concentrating, or trying to think up a solution to the problem at hand, but more as if he was puzzled by something. My mother waited for a long, long time before she broke the silence.

"Hank," my mother asked, "where are we going?"

My father started, as if someone had woken him from a nap. He looked over at my mother. He seemed to be trying to arrive at a decision.

"We can't go south," he said. "It only takes one phone call and they'll have someone checking every car on the way to Calgary."

My mother had no idea what was happening, but she found this immensely logical.

"So," she said. "We won't go south."

"Same thing with east or west," my father said. "The only way to get out of town is along Jasper Avenue, and they'll have that covered as well."

"That only leaves one direction, Hank," my sensible mother said.

Her remark had an immediate effect on my father, who broke out in a grin. "Exactly," he said. "We'll head for the North." He leaned over to give my mother a kiss on the cheek, started up the engine, swung the car around, and headed up Ninety-seventh Street. A decision had been made. They were going north.

Here's what my father hadn't told my mother. Although a position with Investors Syndicate had brought my parents to Edmonton from Regina, my father hadn't lasted long at that job. He was a good salesman, my father, but with one child to support and another on the way, he believed he needed a faster way of making money than selling insurance door-to-door. (Investors Syndicate is still around, although it's now called Investors Group, the expression "syndicate" having taken on negative connotations. My father always maintained it was the Mob that got the company to change its name, since the Mafia was not keen on being associated with life insurance.)

Two blocks away from MacDougall Court, a new office tower was under construction. The garage my father parked his car in was west of the building, and he used to stop in and chat with

Ned, the night watchman, on his way home from making his rounds. One night, he cajoled Ned into letting him into the building. He got a complete tour of what would obviously be much-in-demand offices when they were completed. He and Ned hit it off, and my dad had this great idea. A real get-rich-quick scheme. Here's how it worked.

My father quit his job with Investors Syndicate, spent most of his last paycheque printing up nice stationery and embossed business cards, and went into the office rental business. He would make a cold call, something he was good at, hand people his card, and offer, as a convenience to his customers, to show them around the new high-rise after hours, so they wouldn't be dis tracted by the construction. If a client liked what he saw, my father would do up a letter of agreement on his stationery, take a small deposit, and wave good-bye, planning to be out of town well before the building was finished. He rented out one corner office to twelve different people. It was easy money, involving very little overhead, unless you counted the cost of the stationery and the business cards and the ten-spot my father slipped the night watchman every time he unlocked the door with a cheerful "Good evening, sir, and how are you today?" The only problem was, construction on the building finished early. A client of my dad's showed up for an unannounced visit, and the next thing you knew, my father was leading his pregnant wife down a slippery fire escape in the middle of the afternoon. In the rain.

My father had met my mother when she was a psychiatric nurse at the mental institute in Weyburn, Saskatchewan. He wasn't a patient, although my mother would often say later that he would have fit right in. My father had tried to crash a party the nurses were throwing at their residence. My mother was at the door, because she'd been chosen to chaperone. She belonged to the Student Christian Movement. She didn't smoke. She didn't drink. She was a responsible person. That's what all the other nurses thought: Louise Bell was responsible. None of them knew that, a few months into her new job, my mother had volunteered to be a test subject in a secret clinical trial on the medical properties of LSD, an experiment that first required her to be certified "of sound mental state" by a panel of psychologists. She received an official document from them pronouncing her sane and stating she was "an ideal candidate."

At the age of eighteen, right before starting nursing school, my mother had also hitchhiked her way across Canada all by herself. She started in Burnaby, British Columbia, where she had been born and raised, and she made it all the way to Toronto, Ontario. She was some impressed by Toronto. She rode the streetcar from one end of Queen Street to the other. She had a sandwich at Lindy's. She walked up and down Yonge Street at night, her head tilted back, staring up at the tallest buildings she'd ever seen. Gawking. Later, her one and only experience with drugs would remind her of all that flashing neon. She made a vow to herself, right then and there, that she was going to move to Toronto someday, live in the middle of the noise and excitement. Today it's hard to think of my mother living in the city, but she was headed for Toronto once. Before she met my father.

My father had been drinking the night he crashed the social the psychiatric nurses were throwing. My mother could smell the alcohol on his breath. Since she was death on drinking, she wouldn't let him in. She was impervious to his charms, although he was a very charming fellow. He tried everything he could, but it was Katy, bar the door, and he wasn't getting past her. She tossed him out of the party, in fact. My mother always said she'd had to throw my father down a flight of stairs, while he maintained he'd slipped. Either way, he seemed to take her rejection as a challenge, because the next day he showed up, sober, looking for his hat. He was carrying a single chrysanthemum, and he presented it to her along with the most heartfelt apology my mother had ever heard.

My father hailed from Radville, Saskatchewan. It's a small town in the southern part of the province, without much in the way of nightlife or opportunities. He got out of there as quickly as he could. At the time he met my mother, he was calling himself a salesman, but he had aspirations to be a minor-league grifter. He had previous experience as an actor, a card shark, a pool hustler and a musician. He had played tenor saxophone in a big band, and he was reputed to be good. He was even better at playing pool, having sometimes made a living at it. His acting was limited to several leading roles in productions for the provincial drama festival, but the experience would definitely come in handy.

At the time he met my mother, my father had already settled on a plan. He wanted to do as little work as possible for as much money as possible. He had spent two years as a teacher, right out of his teens, having gone to Normal School the summer he graduated high school. He was seventeen years old when he was assigned to the proverbial one-room schoolhouse in the middle of nowhere. But teaching was hard, and it was not a way to make money. My father was as sharp as the edge of a knife, and he could probably have been successful in any line of work, providing no actual work was involved.

So—those are my parents. That's my mother and that's my father. You have to imagine them as they were. My father, tall and thin as a rail, with a ready smile and a neatly maintained pencil-thin moustache already a few years out of style. He wasn't quite Clark Gable, but on a good day he might manage David Niven. Only taller. My mother was short where he was tall, round where he was thin. She also had a great smile, but she wasn't as eager to share it with strangers.

And four years later, there they sit, in the 1953 two-toned Mercury Zephyr, having made it as far as the town of Peace River. In those days, you could drive from Edmonton to Peace River in about nine hours, and that's what they'd done, pushing on through the night and running out of gas in the early hours of the morning. The hill leading into Peace River was incredibly steep, and they'd coasted their way into town. My father had parked the Zephyr right downtown, and they'd managed a few hours of fitful sleep.

It was rather tense in the car. My brother, having slept through the journey, was now awake, hungry and uncharacteristically cranky. My mother, having endured a silent and potentially dangerous trip, was now looking for some answers. My father was preoccupied with the fact that they would soon be out of cash. He had some money in his wallet, and a few dollars squirrelled away in his shaving kit, but that was it. He had no intention of stopping at a local branch of the Dominion Bank to empty out their account; that money, he figured, was well and truly gone. He was wrong about this, but then he was wrong about a lot of things. The proceeds of his minor crime spree would sit there until the year 2000, when I read an article about a Bank of Canada Web site where you could look up inactive accounts. Sure enough, an on-line search revealed a chequing account in the name of Henry Clark Ferguson, with a held balance of $1,179.48. That would have been a tidy sum in 1959.

Here's what my father didn't know: nobody was chasing them. His bank records were never examined. His con wasn't a big enough deal to warrant a large-scale investigation. The police looked into the matter, the owners of the building paid back most of the deposit money, and some of the prospective tenants ended up renting office space after all. The whole thing blew over. It fell into the category of petty crime. The building owners didn't even fire Ned, the night watchman, although he probably had a few sleepless nights. I don't know what kind of story he cooked up to cover his involvement in the scheme, but my father could no doubt have come up with a much better one to get them both off the hook. If he'd stayed around, he could probably have talked his way out of trouble. At the very least, he could safely have headed east to Winnipeg or west to Vancouver. The guilty man flees where no one pursues.

Back in Peace River, my mother had a thousand questions for my father. She started with the most basic one.

"Hank," she said, "what are we doing here?"

My father didn't have an answer, other than to explain that "here" was as far as they'd been able to go.

"Hank," my mother asked, "what happened in Edmonton?"

My father did have an answer to this, only he didn't feel like sharing it at that moment.

Finally my mother asked the biggest question. She'd been holding off on it, because she was afraid of what the answer might be. "Hank," she asked, "what are we going to do now?"

three

TRUE NORTH

eople were starting to stare. The town of Peace River was waking up, and folks were heading to work. It seemed as if most of them were walking right by my parents and peering into the car. My father had coasted the Zephyr to a stop in the middle of the night. Now, in daylight, people were wondering why he had parked his automobile in the centre of the only park in town.

My father broke into a huge smile. My mother thought it was because he liked all the attention, but really he was smiling because she'd finally asked him a question he could answer.

"Louise," my father said, "this is what we're going to do. I'm going to walk over to that garage and buy some gas. I'm going to bring it back here in a jerry can. I'm going to put it in the tank of the car. Then we're going to go and have breakfast."

"All right. That sounds good. And after that?"

"After that, we're going to take a drive. We'll take a look around and find us a nice motel to stay in."

"All right. And after that?"

"Then we'll probably go have lunch. I think I saw a Chinese place on Main Street."

And that's what they did. They ended up at the Bide-Away Motel, up on the hill leading out of town. The motel is still there, although they've fixed it up some over the years. They have a sign offering colour television now. It was brand-new in 1959, and it didn't need the lure of television to be considered an attractive place to stay. My father could have found cheaper accommodations, but he wanted to make sure my mother felt comfortable, and that he had the situation under control. The room was cozy enough, it was certainly a big improvement over their place back in Edmonton, and it was a bargain at nine dollars a night.

The motel's rates were reasonable, but they still represented my parents' first encounter with the extra costs incurred in living in the North. Luckily, my father kept unused cheques from closed bank accounts for just such a situation. He had already written a cheque at the gas station, and now he wrote one to pay for their room. They went for Chinese food. He paid by cheque. After lunch, he took my mother and my brother back to the motel.

"Hank," my mother asked when she realized he wasn't taking off his coat, "where do you think you're going?"

"Out," said my father. "Don't worry, I'll be back soon."

Up to this point, my mother had been careful not to let anything get her down. She was trying to look at the trip as a big adventure, one they'd laugh at together in years to come. But that changed when my father stepped out the door of the motel. She went to the window to watch him leave. She was convinced she was never going to see him again. She burst into tears, clutching my brother, and for a second or two she contemplated running after her husband. Then she made a decision to calm down. She was pregnant, she reminded herself. Hormones and such. And her morning sickness was acting up again. She took another pill and decided to have a rest. She even managed to have a chuckle over how silly she was being.

"Imagine," she told my brother. "I was worried your father was going to leave us. Isn't that the silliest thing you've ever heard?"

My brother, true to his nature, simply smiled.

As it happened, my father was, at that same moment, trying to convince himself to leave his wife and son. Turn left and keep heading north. Pick up some work along the way, maybe try to get into a card game or two. Shoot a little pool. He was on the run, and he'd be able to move faster without a wife and kid holding him back. Besides, he reasoned, they'd be better off without him. How? Well, let's see. My mother had a family. They weren't that far away, just one province over. Sure. She could contact her parents, get them to send her some money, bring her home . . . But it didn't work. He couldn't come up with a workable solution. At least, he couldn't come up with one that didn't make him a horrible, horrible person, and he wasn't used to thinking of himself in quite that negative a manner. If he had more money, my father thought, he could make sure my mother was looked after before he took off. Then again, if he had more money, he wouldn't be thinking about taking off. So instead of turning left, he turned right, headed back towards the downtown corridor of Peace River, and did something he hadn't done for a long time. He went to find himself a bar.

My father had made my mother a promise. He had told her he was never going to drink again. Or, to be exact, that he would never have another drink as long as they were together. He had religiously attended meetings of Alcoholics Anonymous, both in Regina and in Edmonton, and whenever he took one of his prospective clients out for dinner to close a deal, he stuck to soda water, citing a stomach ailment. He had promised my mother he wouldn't drink, and he was true to his word. The events of the past twenty-four hours had left him with a powerful thirst, however, and that thirst allowed him to spot a loophole in the agreement.

He had promised my mother he would stop drinking *as long as they were together.* Well, wasn't he contemplating leaving her? Didn't that give him the right to have a drink? It was either that or try to track down a local chapter of AA, and he wasn't sure a town this size would have one. Besides, he'd been sober for over two years, with the medallions to show for it. What harm could a drink or two do? Might help him concentrate. He spotted a sign for a licensed room, pulled into a parking spot off Main Street, got out of the car. My father squared his shoulders, took a deep breath, and stepped into the Bruin Inn, a notorious watering hole even by the admittedly low standards of the time. He was ready to do some serious drinking.

"I'm sorry, we're not open yet." That would be the proprietor, a little man with a magnificent comb-over whose name has been lost to history.

"Oh." My father stood in the doorway, blinking, confused, not sure which direction to turn. Having decided to fall off the wagon, he was stunned to be stymied by something as simple as the local liquor hours. He honestly didn't know what to do. His instinctive charm deserted him.

"Well," he asked, and he layered the question with as much sarcasm as possible, "where can a fellow go to get a drink in this town?" He had almost said "one-horse town" but changed his mind at the last second. Which, as it turned out, was a good thing.

"Close the door, you're letting the heat out."

My father made no response to this reply, since it hadn't really answered his question.

"Look," said the proprietor, "come in or go out, but close the door."

My father, being out of options, decided to come all the way into the tavern. He let the door thunk shut softly behind him.

"Only place you could get a drink at this hour," said the proprietor, finally having gotten around to my father's question, "is the Windsor Arms. And that's back down the hill."

My father may have made a move as if to leave, but he was likely only shifting his shoulders under his damp overcoat. It had started to rain again.

"You don't want to go there, though," continued the proprietor. He may have been trying to stop my father from leaving, but it's just as likely that he didn't want the door to open again so soon and let in the cold and damp.

"And why's that?"

"This time of day, it's all Indians and alcoholics," said the barman, going on to display a higher level of erudition than his racial politics would suggest. "But that's redundant. Most of the Indians are drunks as well."

My father had a joke for this. He had a joke for most occasions. And although I would like to believe that a part of him was offended by the proprietor's easy bigotry, I don't imagine he gave it a second thought. He shrugged off his coat and headed for a seat at the bar.

"You know the difference between a drunk and an alcoholic?"

"No sir, I do not."

"Drunk doesn't have to go to all those goddamned meetings."

Now this was an old joke, even at the time, but an old joke that finds a new audience will often go over gangbusters. The little bartender thought it was the funniest thing he'd ever heard. He doubled over laughing, and his artfully maintained comb-over bounced up and down on his head like a greasy black spring. My father couldn't take his eyes off it. It was everything he could do to look the little man in the eye when the man reached under the counter and poured my father . . . a cup of coffee.

"That's a good one," the proprietor said, sliding the cup along the bar with a flourish. "That's a real good one."

My father wanted to see the helmet of hair dance again, so he tried another.

"Guy walks by a bar, sees a sign in the window that says 'All you can drink for one dollar,'"—he paused for a sip of coffee before delivering the punch line—"goes up to the bartender and says, 'I'll have two dollars' worth.'"

"I don't get it." No laughter from the little man this time, no acrobatics from his hair, just puzzlement.

"See," said my father, "he could drink as much as he wanted to, but he wanted to drink twice as much as he wanted to."

"I still don't get it." The proprietor had a point. A joke is either funny or not funny. It doesn't improve if you have to explain it. "I mean, that's a hell of a bargain. All you can drink for only a buck? You'd lose your shirt."

"Yeah, I guess you're right."

"You might as well give the booze away."

"I guess." My father was beginning to regret his decision to stay at the Bruin Inn. He figured that second joke would have killed them down the street at the Windsor Arms.

"I mean, a fellow who did that, shoot, he'd be out of business in a week."

My father was on the verge of saying something rude or sarcastic, or both, when fate stepped in and the conversation took another turn.

"What's a well-dressed young fellow like you doing looking for a drink at two o'clock in the afternoon for, anyways?"

It was a good question, and my father decided it needed a good answer. He told a tale, and it was a clever one, being very close to the actual events that had occurred. Whenever he was telling somebody a story, he would keep as close to the truth as possible, that sort of verisimilitude often making the difference between a successful lie and one that fails.

So he told a story about a young husband and father, with one child already and another on the way, who had left a well-paying sales position in Edmonton and packed up his family and headed north on the promise of a highly paid job waiting for him at the other end of the trail. He was lied to, mister, there was no job waiting for him, and there's nothing worse than being lied to, right, especially when you're an honest person. Like the two of us. Now here he was, almost out of money. He could barely afford to pay for a motel, let alone keep the family fed and healthy. He was at the end of his rope, mister, and that's why he needed a drink. He wasn't proud of himself, and he felt that he'd been lucky with his choice of tavern, because he was, much to his own surprise, going to keep his promise to his good wife never to touch alcohol again.

It was a touching story. The little balding bartender went soft around the eyes a few times when the subject of wife and kids came up. My father was probably setting him up for a loan. After that tale of tears, the barman was sure to cough up a few dollars.

"Salesman, eh?" the bartender commiserated. "That's too bad. Not a lot of call for your line in these parts. It's too damn bad."

My father took a breath, probably readying himself to move in and put the touch on the little fellow, when the proprietor continued.

"It's too bad you're not a teacher by trade. The Peace River separate schools are desperate for teachers."

My mother heard my father drive up in the car. He was just in time. She'd started worrying again. She had good reason to be concerned. Her husband had left her and her baby alone right after lunch, and now it was dark, nighttime really, way past the dinner hour. What if he was gone forever? What if she'd been abandoned? The thought made her angry, and, to take her mind off it, she'd tried to figure out a strategy. She had already come up with several options, most of them involving throwing herself on the mercy of local churches and charities, when my father returned. She was furious, naturally. She threw open the door of the motel room at the exact same moment that the car door slammed shut. The noise made them both jump. Which made my father laugh. Which made my mother angrier.

"Isn't that the damndest thing," my father said. "You'd think both those doors banging at the same time would only be twice as loud as one of them, but they really made a racket, didn't they?"

My mother was having none of this. "Where have you been? I'm worried sick."

"Pack up the boy, Louise."

"We're leaving again?"

This response confused my father. Why would they leave a perfectly fine motel, when the night was already paid for?

"No, we're going out for Chinese."

"Twice in one day?"

"Why not? We're celebrating."

"And what," said my mother, in a dangerous tone of voice, "could we possibly be celebrating?"

My father approached her warily, this not being quite the welcome he'd anticipated.

"Well," he said, "let's see. I was thinking we had a lot of things to celebrate."

"Henry," my mother said—she was really, *really* angry—"we drove here through a rainstorm. We're in the middle of nowhere. You uproot our lives, then you go off and leave the baby and me to ourselves while you're out doing who knows what. I've been a good sport for long enough. I'm well overdue for an explanation."

"Louise," my father said, "I've got a job."

Not only a job, either. He had also found them a place to stay. And he'd done it in one day. After hearing about the tragic shortage of schoolteachers in the Peace River Separate School District, my father had driven over to the district offices and talked his way into a meeting with the district superintendent, a tall, colourless man who had also, coincidentally, done some dramatic rearranging of his hairline. This left my father a tad nonplussed, but he was still able to spin out a tale, once again sticking close to facts. This time, it was a story about a young husband and father, a teacher by profession, a Catholic, even, who was vacationing with his wife and family—one kid, another one on the way—and had fallen in love with the North. The superintendent hired him on the spot.

Now, I'm sure my father fudged his educational experience a little bit during their meeting, as well as his religious affiliation, but he wouldn't have had to. The Peace River Separate School District was that desperate for teachers. Not in the town of Peace River, though, which was unfortunate, because my father had thought it would be the perfect place to hole up for a while. The Peace River Separate School District covered an immense area, reaching all the way to the territorial border, and where they could really use someone of my father's qualifications, it seemed, was at the Indian school in Fort Vermilion. My father had no idea where that was, so the superintendent pulled down a wall map.

"This is where you are now," he said, pointing at Peace River with a ruler.

"And Fort Vermilion is where, exactly?"

The ruler began moving north on the map. "Look up," said the superintendent, "look all the way up."

My father was explaining this to my mother over a meal at the Golden Dragon Chinese and Canadian Café. He was holding my brother Dan on his lap, bouncing him up and down. "They need teachers so bad, they want me to start right away."

"I thought you hated teaching," my mother said.

"I do, but this is a temporary situation. We're going to go up for a few months, a year at the most."

"And then?"

"Then I'll come up with another plan."

"And where are we going to live?"

"That's the best part. The school district provides housing. They're going to put us up in something called a teacherage."

"Which is what, exactly?"

"It's a house, Louise," my father said. "We're going to live in a house."

There was something important that my father didn't bother to tell my mother that evening. The superintendent of separate schools, his unfortunate choice of hairstyles notwithstanding, had tried to talk my father out of taking the job.

"It's a hell of a long way to go, Henry, especially with a young child."

"And another one on the way," my father added.

"Ever had any dealings with the Indians?"

"I taught in Saskatchewan," my father said, avoiding an out-and-out lie.

"Then I don't have to tell you," the superintendent said.

"Tell me what?" my father thought, but out loud he said, "I know what you're trying to say." This is a very successful tactic to use when you have no idea what the other person is talking about. It encourages them to keep talking until you figure things out.

"And the accommodations are a little, well, rustic."

"All part of the northern experience."

"Henry, this is about as far away from anyplace as you'll ever get."

"You make it sound like the end of the earth."

"Oh, it's not the end of the earth," the superintendent said as he slid a contract across the desk for my father to sign. "But you can see it from there."

The contract came with a cheque for resettlement and the first installment of what was then known as the Hardship Posting Allowance. My father concluded the meeting in time to get to the bank and cash the cheque. Barely. They had already locked the doors, but he talked his way into the branch, and that was one of the reasons he'd been so late in getting back to my mother. He didn't tell her about their sudden windfall, though. Since he didn't worry her with talk about money when they didn't have any, he figured he shouldn't bring it up now. If she started going on about selling the car again, that's when he would tell her they were flush.

My mother couldn't have been more pleased with how things were working out. She was especially looking forward to living in a house again. My father had been hired with instructions to re-port to work immediately, so after one night in the Bide-Away Motel, they were on their way.

Fort Vermilion is 526 miles north of Edmonton. If you took the trip today, you'd find that most of the highway is in pretty good shape. You can go as far as High Level before you run out of pavement. The roads were more demanding when my parents made the trip. It didn't help that the rain seemed to be following them, though as they made their way north it changed into sleet and then snow. The roads also got worse and worse as they went. Blacktop gave way to gravel, the gravel became dirt, and just as they reached High Level the dirt road changed into a single muddy and slippery rut. It looked, thought my mother, like the last wagon trail left in the West, and she could imagine a proces-sion of Red River carts slowly making their way along it. My

father was thinking less romantic thoughts. He was thinking he
had made the worst mistake of his life.

The trip to High Level took them most of the day. They
would gladly have checked into a motel and started fresh in the
morning, but there were no accommodations to be had. High
Level, at that time, was more of an intersection than a town.
There was a gas station, a coffee shop, and a shack that served as
the northern terminus of the Greyhound bus line. That was it.
My father double-checked his directions with the fellow pumping
their gas, happy to learn their destination wasn't much farther
away. Even given the condition of the roads, my father felt they
should be able to make Fort Vermilion in an hour or two. He paid
for the gas and thanked the attendant.

"Was you planning to make the Fort tonight?"

My father had been about to drive off. But there was something in the man's voice that made him get out of the car,
carefully closing the door to protect my mother from any
bad news.

"I was hoping to," he said.

"Well, you'll have to make pretty good time, or you'll miss the
last ferry."

"Ferry?"

"Yeah, sure, you have to cross the river to get into Fort
Vermilion."

"Isn't there a bridge?"

"Why would anybody bother building a bridge over there?"

My father chose not to debate the point. He did want to get
one pivotal piece of information, however.

"What time," my father asked, "does the ferry stop running?"

"Ten o'clock, on the nose," the attendant said. "If you miss it,
they don't start up again until morning."

My father thought about this warning. They'd left Peace
River at seven in the morning, and it had taken twelve hours to

get to High Level. That meant they had three hours available to them to travel the fifty-five miles to Fort Vermilion. My father thought this was eminently achievable and told the gas station attendant. The man smiled and retreated to the warmth of the station, calling to my father over his shoulder as he left.

"Well, good luck to you," he said. "I hope you make it." Adding, as my father was getting back into the car, "That road isn't in very good shape."

They missed the ferry. It took them more than three hours to make the forty-mile trip to the landing where the ferry docked. Nothing they had experienced so far had prepared them for the condition the road was in. The Red River settlers would have turned around and gone home. My parents didn't have any choice; they pushed on, my father driving as fast as he could while still being mindful of safety. On good stretches, he was able to push the Zephyr up to twenty-five miles an hour. Then the road would buckle and crack, occasionally disappearing, and they would have to slow down to a crawl. They finally reached the crossing, only there was no ferry waiting for them, just a single light and a sign telling them they were in the right place. My father turned off the ignition and slumped forward, his head coming to rest on the steering wheel. He had reached his limit.

My mother tried to come up with a course of action.

"Hank," she asked, "do you think we missed the last ferry?"

My father didn't lift his head. "Yes," he said.

"Are you sure?"

In reply, my father held up his wrist so she could read the time.

"Well, we can't spend the night in the car," my mother said. "It's too cold."

My father grunted his agreement.

"And I don't think we're up to driving back."

My father shook his head without lifting it from the steering wheel.

"Well," my mother said, "here's what I think we should do . . . what's that noise?"

In later years, my mother would claim that, despite the hopeless situation they found themselves in, she had come up with a workable solution she was about to reveal to my father. She never went into the details, so we'll have to take her word for it. In any case, my father didn't get to hear her suggestion. Which may have been a good thing. He was under considerable pressure, and he might have reacted badly.

"What noise?" my father asked, this time summoning the energy to lift his head.

"Can't you hear that?"

They were both quiet for a moment. Still. Listening. Then my father exploded out of the car. Coming through the darkness they could hear the sound of a motor chugging and the slapping of a paddlewheel. It was the last ferry. And it was the best sound they could have heard.

My father rushed down to greet it, waving his arms in the air even though no one could see him, a big stupid grin on his face. The ferry got close enough for him to see the light from the cabin, then the motor stopped and the boat glided to the shore.

The door to the wheelhouse opened, and out stepped the biggest Indian my father had ever seen. That's literally what he was thinking when he first laid eyes on Bud Peyen, "That's the biggest Indian I've ever seen," only to amend it after a moment to "Never mind the Indian, that's the biggest person I've ever seen." Bud Peyen was an imposing sight, especially coming off the deck of the ferry.

"Hello," my father said. "We thought we'd missed you."

"Hmmm." Bud Peyen wasn't much for small talk, especially with people he didn't know. Especially with white people he didn't know. He started tying the ferry up to the dock, which was confusing to my father. He didn't know much about boats, though, so he watched Bud work. My mother knew slightly more about boats, and it sure looked to her like that big fellow was putting the ferry away for the night. She left my brother in the car and got out and told my father this. He put her theory to the test. He walked up to where Bud Peyen was doing something to the front of the ferry with padlocks and asked the obvious question.

"Excuse me, is this the last ferry?"

"Depends."

"Depends?" My father was beginning to wonder if he was going to get a straight answer from anybody who lived in the North. "Depends on what?"

"Well," said Bud Peyen, "it's the last ferry for the night, but it's not the last ferry for the season."

My father gave my mother a look of triumph. See? It was the last ferry for the night, what could be simpler than that? Everything was going to work out. My mother spoiled his mood by asking her own question.

"Are you," she said, "going to take us across the river?"

"Nope."

"Why not?" my father asked, dumbfounded.

" 'Cause I'm the last ferry coming from that direction." Bud could see that he needed to elaborate. "The last ferry going *to* that direction was at ten o'clock."

My mother could see my father was angry enough to do or say something that wouldn't be a smart idea out here in the middle of nowhere, especially with a man that size. Of course they were perfectly safe to say anything, Bud Peyen wouldn't even have raised his voice, but they couldn't know that at the time.

"I'm sorry," said my mother, "but there has to be some way for us to cross. My husband is the new schoolteacher, and we have to get to our—what's it called, Hank?"

"A teacherage." He said that through gritted teeth. He really was on the verge of doing or saying something inappropriate.

"Can you help us?"

"Depends."

"On what?" My mother jumped in quickly on that one.

"If you want to cross the river, I can't help you." Bud was being extremely patient; he could tell my parents were tired and a little testy. "If you want to go to where you're staying, I can help you."

This left both my mother and my father at a complete loss for words.

Bud Peyen sighed. He obviously hadn't made himself clear.

"You're the new schoolteacher?" My father nodded. "And you're his wife?" My mother nodded. "See, the school is on that side of the river." He pointed to help them understand. "House they've put you up in is on this side of the river."

It took a while for the information to sink in. Finally, my mother broke the silence.

"You can take us to where we're supposed to go?"

"Sure."

"Let me get this straight," said my father. "What would have happened if we'd crossed the river and gone into town?"

Bud Peyen shrugged. This was almost too obvious to merit a reply.

"Somebody would have pointed you in the right direction." He snapped off the light in the wheelhouse. "Everybody knows you're coming."

Bud Peyen turned and walked to his pickup truck. My parents exchanged a look, then scrambled to get to their car so they could follow him. Before she got in, my mother had a thought. She called out to Bud Peyen.

"This teacherage," she said, "is it nice?"

"Depends," said Bud Peyen, "on what you're used to."

four

*M*EDICINE
MAN

Since *my father and mother* and brother had ended
up in Fort Vermilion, it seemed only decent for
me to join them. My dramatic birth was fol-
lowed by some dramatic early days. I had underdeveloped lungs
and all sorts of things wrong with my stomach and intestines. I
couldn't breathe. That was the real problem.

We did a lot of travelling together, my mother and I. By the
time I was nine months old, the two of us had been flown down to
Peace River three different times on what they called "air evacs."
The first time was to insert a piece of stainless steel mesh in my
stomach, to allow my muscles some support while they were developing. The second time was to repair a hernia caused by the
previous operation. And the third time down I was placed in an
iron lung for a weekend, while the doctors tried to figure out what
was going on with my breathing. I wasn't doing enough of it.
After much consultation, and not a little hand-wringing, they
gave my mother the following diagnosis: we don't know what's
wrong and we don't know how to fix it.

My mother and I were sent home, with the implied understanding that she shouldn't get too attached to me. I had what appeared to be severe asthmatic symptoms, but the traditional treatments were not working. We did discover that I was deathly allergic to penicillin when an attempt to treat me with antibiotics failed miserably. I ended up in a brief coma. This was handled by the fine medical staff at St. Theresa's Catholic Hospital in beautiful downtown Fort Vermilion, so no airplane was required on that occasion.

After their first winter, my parents were tired of the commute across the river. My father, for reasons of his own, had refused an offered teacherage in town in favour of building a house. Maybe he felt a family of four needed more room than the cramped teacherages offered. More likely, he didn't want to live next to his colleagues in education, whom he found annoying. My parents bought some land, and my father spent the first part of his second summer in Fort Vermilion clearing the trees. Bud Peyen did most of the actual work. My mother provided the architectural design. She had made a charcoal drawing of her dream home when she was a little girl, and it was still in her possession. She unpacked it and unfolded it and showed it to my father.

"Make it look like that," she said.

"Just like that?"

"Exactly like that," my mother said, "only bigger."

The house was built on a foundation of split-beam logs. It was sturdy, but you couldn't find a single corner that was perfectly square. There wasn't much skilled labour involved in its construction. Bud Peyen had helped to build a few houses over the years, but he was no master carpenter. My father was afraid of heights and remarkably clumsy with a hammer. Work went slowly. My mother maintains the house would never have been finished if it weren't for the assistance of an elderly Mennonite named John

Wiebe, who passed by in his horse-drawn wagon every morning on his way to the Hilltop Mission. After watching the progress for most of the summer, he took pity on my father and showed up one day with his tools. He became the foreman of the project, and the three men finished the house before the first snow.

The house was two storeys high, 24′ × 24′ square, with a sharply sloped roof to keep off the snow but no electricity or plumbing. The toilet was outside, fifty feet from the kitchen door, and my mother decorated the inside of the outhouse with colour pages from Pogo comics. The floor of the house was plywood, except in the kitchen, where it had a layer of battleship linoleum. The stairway to the second floor wasn't quite complete. There was lots to do before you could call the house a home, but my father still picked up my mother in his arms and carried her across the threshold.

"Well," he said, "it isn't much, but it's ours."

"I think it's beautiful," my mother said.

They probably kissed. They were romantic back in those days. The house had been carefully cleaned to keep the sawdust from interfering with my breathing, and my parents were relieved when I made it to my first birthday.

Many naysayers, meaning medical professionals, hadn't believed this would happen, and my family celebrated the occasion in a proper manner. My mother baked a cake, my father borrowed a camera from Scott Wagner, the manager of the Hudson's Bay store (who also threw in a free roll of film), and I stopped breathing. Again. My father squeezed in one photo of me sitting in front of the cake, my eyes wide as I stared at the single candle, but then it was time for another panicked trip to the hospital. It was the usual routine: a little oxygen, a couple of blood tests. What made this trip different from our previous outings was that my brother wasn't brought down to St. Theresa's to wait. Instead, my dad dropped my mother and me off, then took Dan over to a neighbour's. This would turn out to be a significant move.

Dan was four years old by now, a quiet, some might say reserved, little fellow. He didn't make friends easily with other children, but my mother had noticed that he got along well with a little girl named Lucy Noskiye, who was a year or two older. They'd met outside the Hudson's Bay store. Lucy had found Dan's blue eyes fascinating, and she was soon carrying him around, smothering him with kisses and treating him like an exotic doll. My mother met Lucy's mother, and they, too, hit it off famously. So when I ended up celebrating my first birthday with yet another emergency trip to the hospital, my mother suggested to my father that he take Dan over to the Noskiyes's place. Neither of my parents would admit to this later, but I always got the feeling they had wanted Dan out of the picture because this attack was severe enough to make it look like my final one. Date of birth: November 3 (or 4), 1959. Date of death: November 3 (or 4, if I hung in past midnight), 1960. Not a lot of mileage there.

While my parents hovered at my bedside, my brother was busy being sad over at the Noskiye house. Lucy's mom picked up on his mood, but she didn't say anything. She was a grownup, and grownups know their way around awkward social situations. Lucy, however, wasn't about to let him off the hook so easily.

"How come you don't want to play?" she asked.

"Because I'm sad," my brother answered.

"How come you're sad?"

"Because my baby brother is sick."

"How come he's sick?"

"Nobody knows." There was a long pause while Dan thought this over. "I think he's going to die."

"Oh." Lucy pondered this statement. "My uncle died," she said, "but he was really old."

"Yeah."

"Isn't your brother a baby?"

"Yeah," Dan said, this time beginning to tear up a bit. "He's a baby."

"Well, you should take him to my grandpa. He'll fix him."

"Really?"

"Oh, yeah. He can fix anybody. Unless they're really old."

Lucy, having solved the problem, then went to tell her mother that something important was going on. The two of them had a conversation in Cree, so Dan didn't know what was being said or decided. But he remembers what happened afterwards. He got bundled back up, along with Lucy, and the two kids and Lucy's mom went for a long walk. Then they got into a truck, then they went for a long drive, then he fell asleep for a while. Then he woke up again, and they were still driving, but this time they were in a different truck. At least, that's how he remembers it. In his defence, he was only four years old at the time. I don't remember a single thing.

Here's what happened at the hospital. It was past midnight, and my father had gone outside for a cigarette. He noticed a rusty, incredibly battered, orange-and-red 1949 International truck pulling into the hospital parking lot. It was moving at quite a clip, and when it skidded to a halt, it threw up gravel and dirt in every direction. The truck was, my father always said, "chock full of Indians." They got out in a hurry and opened the passenger door. Out stepped, and again this is how my father told the story, "the oldest Indian I'd ever seen in my life." The group made their way through the front doors; my father walked over to the riverbank and flipped his cigarette into the water. He watched as the glow from the ember floated down out of sight, listened to see if he could hear it hiss out, and tried to work up enough courage to rejoin his wife in the emergency room. St.

Theresa's didn't have an emergency ward, but they did have one room dedicated to traumas and severe medical problems. The Indians called it "the room where people go to die."

In the room, my mother was holding my hand or stroking my cheek or singing me a song or doing whatever parents do when they are desperately afraid for their children. She doesn't remember much about what she was doing, but she never forgot what happened next.

There was a commotion outside the emergency room; one of the doctors was yelling something. Something like "You can't go in there," or "That's not allowed," or "Get out." There were sounds of a struggle, and then the door to the room was wrenched open, and the first thing my mother saw was my brother Dan, not safely at the home of a playmate but here at the hospital, surrounded by a horde of Indians, none of whom she'd ever met before. And, man, were those Indians loud. They were chattering away in Cree, talking a mile a minute, and then, just like that . . . silence.

That's when Lucy Noskiye's great-grandfather—it could even have been her great-great-grandfather—entered the room. He was plenty old, in any case. He was already rumoured to be over a hundred, and would go on to live for another fifteen years, so who knows? He was, in fact, the last of the old Medicine Men, the end of a line of traditional aboriginal healers that stretched back a thousand years or more. Unlike regular doctors, Medicine Men were responsible for the spiritual health and well-being of their community, not just the physical. They could make objects move if they had to, and the really good ones could control the weather.

None of this was known to my mother, but the sudden silence and the reverence that the rest of the Indians showed for the old man were enough to alert her that something was up. The old man didn't look particularly spiritual, or even powerful. He was a short, bandy-legged, incredibly ancient man wearing dusty blue jeans, a faded plaid shirt and a cowboy hat. He couldn't have looked less like my mother's concept of a Medicine Man if he'd tried.

The old man said something in Cree, and a younger man, in his mid-forties, stepped forward to translate.

"This is Augustus Noskiye. I'm his grandson. He says you've got a sick boy."

My mother didn't have a chance to respond. Dr. Vogt marched into the room, and it was obvious he was some mad. Dr. Vogt had finished thirty-ninth out of a class of forty at McGill Medical School. This was why he had ended up at St. Theresa's. He was an insecure man, which he covered up by being loud, brusque and rude.

"All right, everybody has to leave. Right now. Out, out, out . . . "

Dr. Vogt made shooing motions with his hands. The Indians didn't say or do anything. They looked over at Augustus Noskiye, who said something in Cree, and they all started talking again at the same time. Dr. Vogt spoke louder and louder to be heard over the noise. He became so frustrated that he started jumping up and down as he yelled at the crowd.

"Get out! Get out, get out, get out!" And so on and so forth.

While this was going on, Augustus Noskiye and his middle-aged grandson had crossed over to take a look at me. I wasn't a pleasant sight, I'm told. I was in an oxygen tent, and my colour wasn't good. Augustus Noskiye leaned in close, then straightened up and said something to his grandson.

"He says your boy is sick, right?"

My mother nodded. It was so noisy she could barely hear herself think.

"My grandfather may be able to help him."

That's when the penny dropped. My mother took another look at the old Indian. He caught her eye. There was something in his face that my mother trusted. Something she recognized, though she couldn't put her finger on what it was.

"Is your grandfather a . . ." She paused. She felt silly asking the question. "Is he, uh, a Medicine Man?"

"You betcha." This was said so simply and with such conviction that she had to believe it. Augustus Noskiye wasn't saying a word, but he kept his gaze level on my mother.

"Can he help my son?"

This required another conversation between grandson and grandfather.

"He says maybe, but he'll have to take a look at him first."

Those words sounded louder than they should have because the room had abruptly gone quiet. My mother turned to see the new chief resident of St. Theresa's General Hospital marching into the room, the crowd parting before him. Dr. Vogt had gone and tattled to his boss.

"What on earth is going on here?"

The man asking that question was Dr. Gopichand Usman, and he was, after Augustus Noskiye, the oldest person in the room. Dr. Usman was a recently retired microsurgeon from Bombay, India. He had taught at prestigious medical schools in England and South Africa, and he hadn't enjoyed his retirement. His wife, tired of his constant ill humour, had suggested that he either take up a hobby or, after fifty years of marriage, file for a divorce. Dr. Usman decided to fulfill a childhood dream of going to Canada's untamed northern wilderness and shooting a moose. He bought a brand-new rifle and a bright orange vest, but he was a terrible hunter.

Despite his credentials and his experience, the only hospital that offered Dr. Usman a job was St. Theresa's. He had been in

Fort Vermilion for six months, and he had already made himself known. He had gone to the hospital board soon after his arrival and laid down the law. They'd responded by putting him in charge of St. Theresa's, which meant Dr. Vogt had been passed over for a long-anticipated promotion.

"What is that man doing to my patient?"

Augustus Noskiye had bent over and was carefully removing me from the oxygen tent when Dr. Usman marched over and grabbed his arm. The crowd literally gasped with shock. Augustus Noskiye shook off Dr. Usman's hand and said something to him, directly to him, in Cree. His grandson translated, but the tone was clear.

"My grandfather says if you lay hands on him again he'll put you in the ground."

"Tell your grandfather if he touches my patient again, I'll see he is put in jail."

"My grandfather wants to know if you're a healer."

"Tell him," said Dr. Usman, "that I'm a doctor."

"My grandfather says he thought a doctor was the same thing as a healer."

"It is, and I am, and he is putting my patient at risk."

"My grandfather says you've put the boy at risk."

"Oh, does he?" Dr. Usman gave a small twitch of his head. "Really? Isn't that interesting."

"My grandfather says it may or may not be interesting, but it is true."

At this moment in the confrontation my mother realized what she'd recognized earlier in Augustus Noskiye.

"You two are the same," she said.

She probably didn't say it out loud. But watching those two old men standing toe to toe, she saw how alike they were. Not physically. Augustus Noskiye was short and skinny and hawk-nosed. Gopichand Usman was tall and round-bellied and bald.

They had different ways of standing, and different ways of using their hands, and different ways of talking. But the men had the same look in their eyes. It was a confidence, almost an arrogance, that came from the knowledge they could beat death. What my mother was watching was a confrontation between European and aboriginal medicine. She stood up and stepped in between the two men.

"That's enough," she said. "Do I have to knock your heads together?"

Dr. Usman reared back, managing to look insulted and amused at the same time. A moment later, once his grandson had finished translating what my mother said, Augustus Noskiye had exactly the same look on his face.

"Dr. Usman," my mother said, "this man is an Indian doctor. He wants to take a look at my son. I have given him my permission. I don't see what harm it could do."

Dr. Usman thought that a witch doctor giving my mother false hope was extremely harmful. But he wasn't a cruel man, and he couldn't think of any way of telling her that. He nodded his assent. Augustus Noskiye took me out of the hospital crib and placed me in my mother's arms. Then he began to poke at me. His movements were economical and brisk. After he finished his examination, he looked grim, and he had a long conversation with his grandson. He was obviously saying something controversial, because the other Indians either looked shocked or nodded in agreement.

"My grandfather wants to know if you wanted this baby."

My mother said later this was the one time in her life when she could have killed someone with her bare hands. Dr. Usman decided that enough was enough.

"You are not only putting my patient at risk, you are upsetting my patient's mother. This is unconscionable. You must leave this instant." He was about to lay hands on Augustus Noskiye for a second time, which would have meant big trouble, when my mother spoke up.

"I love my son. Do you understand me? I have wanted him and waited for him my entire life. If you're not going to help, then go away. I don't need you here if you're not going to help us."

This was duly translated, and Augustus Noskiye made a lengthy reply.

"My grandfather says he's sorry. The reason he asked is that this boy has been poisoned. It is some poison that you took while you were carrying him. Now he believes you didn't know you took this poison. He feels maybe someone evil slipped it into your tea."

"Poison?" Dr. Usman was back to being a disbeliever. "Good grief."

"Dr. Usman," my mother said, "please be quiet."

She couldn't look at Augustus Noskiye, because she was about to ask a really important question, and she wasn't sure she wanted to hear the answer. She talked directly to the translator.

"Can you ask your grandfather, since he knows what is wrong, if he thinks he can help my son?"

There was a long consultation between Augustus and his grandson.

"My grandfather says he can only help the boy if the boy wants to keep living."

Dr. Usman had reached his limit. "And how on earth is he going to determine that?"

The answer to his question came immediately. Without warning, Augustus Noskiye took me from my mother's arms, holding me by the heels and the back of my head. He lifted me straight up until his arms were fully extended. I arched my back to keep from falling.

"Jesus Christ. What the hell is going on here?"

That was my father. He had made his way through the crowd inexplicably gathered in the emergency room just in time to watch some old man snatch his son up in a very dangerous manner. To be honest, he was more concerned about my mother being upset; as far as I went, he was already preparing himself for the inevitable. He started to cross the room, but there were all of a sudden too many Indians in his way. Then he felt something tugging at his pant leg, and he looked down to see his older son staring up at him.

"Dad," said my big brother, Dan, "it's okay."

"Your boy wants to live. That's good."

That was the translator. Since Augustus Noskiye hadn't said a word, this couldn't be taken as a professional opinion. The old Medicine Man looked at my father, then at my mother, and then, carefully, at me. He said something, and the room became quiet again.

"My grandfather says you aren't Indians."

"No," my mother said, "we're not."

"So your boy has no Indian in him." It wasn't a question.

"No, of course not."

"Well, you know, this is old-time Indian medicine. It only works if you're an Indian."

My father would have said something, probably something that would have worsened the situation, but my mother spoke first.

"Are you saying you won't treat my son because he's not an Indian?"

There was a short conversation, almost an argument, between August Noskiye and his grandson. Then the Medicine Man turned back to my mother, and his face wrinkled up in a smile. His grandson translated.

"He says no problem; we'll turn him into an Indian."

"When will you do that?"

"Oh, don't worry. First we'll fix him, then we'll change him."

And that's what happened. Augustus Noskiye fixed me. He had my parents check me out of the hospital and take me to his house, where his wife made everybody tea, including Dr. Usman, who had given in to his professional curiosity. I was carried out back into a small, solidly built cabin where the Medicine Man did some things with steam and smoke and herbs and other stuff. Nobody knows, because nobody else was allowed into that cabin. He filled a Mason jar with some foul-smelling green liquid that my parents were supposed to give me three times a day. And that was that. My mother asked if she needed an appointment to bring me back, and she was surprised by the answer.

"My grandfather says give him the medicine and he'll get better."

My parents both tried some of the green liquid when they got home. It tasted as bad as it smelled, but it didn't make them sick. So what the hell, they figured, it couldn't hurt. They'd find out later that the green stuff was a medicinal tea. The biggest ingredient in it was rat root, which grows in swamps and sloughs and is the foundation for a lot of traditional medicine in northern Alberta and Saskatchewan. Rat root is distributed in dried short plugs that look like little pieces of driftwood. Chew it and it cures toothaches and headaches. Grind it into a powder, add a few other herbs and plants, and it makes a poultice that heals wounds without a scar. For stomach ailments, you boil it and drink the water hot. For other ailments, the rat root gets boiled along with other ingredients, which, depending on what you're trying to cure, could include anything from wild peppermint to pine needles.

Dr. Usman was fascinated by my recovery, and he sent a sample of the green medicine off to be analyzed at the University of Alberta. The report came back months after I finished my treatment. My medicine contained a natural opiate, the report said, something with steroidal qualities, and something else they weren't able to identify but were eager to explore further. Could Dr. Usman send them another sample? He didn't, though. By this point, Dr. Usman was consulting with Augustus Noskiye about many of his patients. The two men didn't become friends, but they did become esteemed colleagues. Having spent his life-time with the scientific method, Dr. Usman decided to treat it as a matter of faith.

"It works or it doesn't work, depending on what you believe," Dr. Usman would say.

Augustus Noskiye and his grandson showed up at our house the summer before I was set to start school. I was six years old then, and they were finally getting around to closing that loop-hole. It was time to turn me into an Indian.

"My grandfather says we got to get it done before he goes to school," the grandson said. "Otherwise it might not take."

They had pulled into our yard in their old truck, and they seemed in a hurry to get going. Augustus Noskiye hadn't stepped out of the cab, and his grandson had politely refused my mother when she offered to make tea. My parents weren't invited to come along, and my father had some concerns about this.

"What, exactly," he said, and he was choosing his words care-fully, "will be involved in this, uh, transformation?"

The grandson translated the question. Augustus Noskiye chuckled and spoke directly to my father.

"He says not to worry, it doesn't hurt or anything," the grand-son translated.

Augustus Noskiye was still chortling to himself as the three of us drove away. My parents were waving good-bye, and he'd wave back at them, then giggle, then wave some more, until he finally turned to me and said something. His grandson was busy making a sharp turn onto the road leading out of town, so I had to wait for him to translate.

"My grandfather says it doesn't hurt to turn into an Indian. But he says it can hurt *being* an Indian."

I had no idea what that meant, so I asked. "What does he mean by that?"

"Don't ask me. He's the one who said it."

The Beaver and Cree used to bury their dead on platforms in the branches of trees. There were practical reasons for this. The frozen ground made it hard to dig graves, and placing the newly deceased up high kept them safe from most scavengers. But the real reason not to bury people was because, when you die, your spirit goes up into the sky. What we call the northern lights is actually the spirits of all the Indians who have passed away, dancing in the heavens. If you go out into the middle of a field when the aurora borealis are in full fiery glory, rub your fingernails together and whistle through your teeth, and the spirits will come closer and dance just for you. If you're lucky enough to see them in the Real North, the True North, you'll get to hear the music they dance to as the northern lights murmur and crackle.

The Elleski Shrine was built into the side of a hill across the river from Fort Vermilion, just beneath a cemetery. The cemetery on top had one or two proper gravesites and a few Christian crosses, but the majority of the plots were Spirit Houses, which is what the Indians called the buildings they erected over their dead. The Spirit Houses ranged in style from miniature log cabins to tiny wood-framed cottages. Most of them had been painted white or covered in mud that had dried the colour of whitewash. All of them had a Spirit Hole. The cemetery was beautiful. It looked like a village of small houses.

We stopped at the Elleski Shrine that day, after I was turned into an Indian. Augustus Noskiye hadn't lied to my parents; the ceremony hadn't hurt at all. They took me to the Sacred Place, and they taught me a song, and then they told me the history of the People. The history took a long time to tell, but it was never boring. A lot of stuff had happened. They made me promise to learn the language and pass it on to my children. That seemed easy enough; I was surrounded by people speaking Cree, and I had already picked up many words. We climbed up from the Sacred Place and sat outside and had some sandwiches. Then we got back in the truck.

"Is it over?" I asked.

"That's it," the grandson said. "My grandfather just wants to make one more stop."

We sat looking at the Elleski Shrine for a long while before the Medicine Man said anything. When he started talking, he spoke so quickly it was hard for his grandson to keep up with him.

"A long time ago, this priest was sent up here to teach everybody about Jesus Christ. He didn't like the Spirit Houses. He said it went against the Church. He hired some men and they knocked down all the Spirit Houses and put all the People in the ground. The next week nobody showed up at his church. And the week after that nobody came again. And that went on for a while, until the Church got rid of this priest. They sent him down south, where he wouldn't have to deal with the People. The next priest built this shrine here for the mother of Jesus Christ. And he put all the Spirit Houses back. He did this by himself. Nobody would help him."

I was listening to Augustus Noskiye tell me something. I knew it was important, and I was trying to figure out what the lesson was.

"That priest was Father Litzler, and he's still here in Fort Vermilion today. That's why we like Father Litzler. And also why Indians should stick together."

Augustus Noskiye and his grandson drove me home after that. There wasn't much conversation, but every once in a while Augustus Noskiye would reach over and mess up my hair. He smiled every time he did this. When we got to my house, they both came in and had tea with my parents.

A few months went by before my father realized he must owe somebody something. He went to Bud Peyen for advice.

"Bud, how does payment work with a Medicine Man?"

"You don't pay them, Hank, you give them a present."

"What kind of present?"

"Tobacco is good."

"I should take him a pouch of tobacco?"

"Jeez, he saved the boy's life, Hank, I'd at least give him a carton of tailor-mades."

five

LOST
BOY

That was the year it snowed every month, even in July. That was the year I became a big brother. My mother had another baby, and that might have been the most exciting thing to happen that year. It wasn't. That was the year Lloyd Loonskin got lost in the woods. And that was the year that Canada threw a party and we weren't invited.

The rest of the country was preparing to celebrate the Centennial. There were going to be fireworks and speeches and a giant get-together in Montreal. The year even had a theme song, Bobby Gimby's ode to one little, two little, three Canadians. Most of Fort Vermilion had never heard the song, though. Our closest radio station was CKYL in Peace River, which played Country music, mainly, sometimes Western. When the atmospheric conditions were right, their signal made it north to us. If you had a radio, you could sing along. If you had electricity.

The town's power supply came from two generators, one of which was turned off every night. Most houses couldn't afford electricity. Even the families who could flip a switch and turn on the lights likely felt that a radio fell into the category of unnecessary luxury item. The folks at the Experimental Farm were there to do scientific research, though, and they had not only had electricity but a big outdoor antenna. They could listen to the radio any time they wanted. Those folks were excited about Expo '67. So were our teachers. So was Scott Wagner, the manager of the Hudson's Bay store, and most of the other people from out.

The rest of us didn't care too much about it. As far as we were concerned, Canada was fictional, a kind of dream. Imagining it was like thinking about England or the United States or Australia or other places we were never going to get to see. It was all the same to us. We didn't even go over to the fairgrounds to watch the Dominion Day show Scott Wagner had organized. Which was just as well. It stormed.

This wasn't a brief snowstorm like the one we'd had in June. This was wind and sleet and temperatures that dropped below freezing. Dan and I had already pulled the insulating hay bales away from the side of the house and built a fort with them, but we had to put them back. My father was annoyed because he had to arrange for Bud Peyen to drop off more firewood, which was an inconvenience and an extra expense. Bud Peyen showed up with some six-foot sections of tree and his crosscut saw, and he and my father went to work. Which is to say, Bud did most of the cutting and my father did most of the talking.

"Snow on Canada's birthday," he said. "What do you think, Bud? Is this a bad omen?"

"I don't know if it's an omen or not, Hank, but we're sure off to a bad start."

July stayed cold. Not cold like in the winter, when people would leave their vehicles running twenty-four hours a day and clouds of diesel fumes stayed close to the ground like fog on the river. Not that cold. But more than cold enough to get everybody complaining.

Nobody in town liked the cold. What was there to like? January and February, the thermometer would slide down to around thirty-five or forty below, then settle there for a month or so. This was called a cold snap. It didn't make any difference if you were measuring the temperature in Celsius or Fahrenheit; it was hateful. You didn't dare go outside without every inch of your body covered, because exposed flesh would freeze in an instant. It was fingers, usually, that would go first. You had to have good gloves. My mother outfitted us all with woollen mitts she bought from a Mennonite lady named Mrs. Wiebe. (No relation to the John Wiebe who had built our house; Wiebe was the equivalent of Smith in the Anabaptist community.) This Mrs. Wiebe was renowned for both the quality of her knitwear and the speed with which she could turn it out. Her mitts were so warm your hands would sweat inside.

Earlier that year, in the middle of a cold snap, during a stretch of record low temperatures, I had taken my mitts off momentarily to get a better purchase on the only swing set in the schoolyard. I froze my right hand onto the metal. This was after classes had ended for the day, and it was already getting dark. The only person available to help was my friend Lloyd Loonskin.

"Hey," I said. "Ouch," I said. "That stings!" And, again, "Hey."

I was trying to get his attention. Lloyd Loonskin was swinging fearlessly from the crossbar twelve feet overhead, and it wasn't easy for him to hear me. I tried yelling, but we were both so muffled up in scarves and toques that communication was difficult. I could barely hear myself.

"Ouch!"

I was much louder this time. Lloyd stopped himself in mid-swing and hung effortlessly from the crossbar.

"What's wrong?"

"I froze my hand, Lloyd. I'm stuck."

Lloyd Loonskin dropped down onto the ground. He made the descent look easy and painless. He floated. His feet barely seemed to touch the ground. The swing set had no actual swings attached; it was supposed to be off-limits to the students until it got replaced or repaired. We weren't holding our breath waiting. It had never, in anybody's recent memory, had swings connected to it. We didn't care. What could you do with a swing? Swing, I guess. That sounded boring. It was more fun to play "Let's climb up to the top and jump off." That was a game Lloyd Loonskin had more or less invented. I was scared of heights, but I was able to conquer my fear long enough to reach the top. My landings, unlike his, weren't easy or painless. I would hit the ground hard enough to make my teeth snap together, and it usually took me a second or two to get my wind back.

"Hey, partner, what's wrong?"

"I told you." I was becoming alarmed at the fact that I couldn't feel my fingers. "I froze my hand."

This earned me a disgusted roll of his eyes. He was completely not impressed.

"Well, what were you taking your mitts off for, anyways?"

I confess that by this point I had tears in my eyes. And it wasn't only from being cold. Since my face was completely wrapped up in a scarf, with my eyes barely visible, I was hoping he wouldn't notice.

No such luck. "Hey, partner . . . you crying?"

"Look, my hand is stuck. You've got to go get some help."

"Just pull it off."

"No. If I pull it off, all the skin is gonna come away."

"Well, so what?"

"Well, I'll bleed all over my coat."

"So?"

"My mom will get mad at me."

Lloyd couldn't argue with that. He didn't have a mother to call
his own, so he placed great importance on mine. In later years,
when he was grown up and living far away, he would sometimes
call her on the phone. Mostly he'd be sober, but sometimes not.
She could always tell when he'd been drinking. He'd call her
"Mommy."

"Well, what do you want me to do?"

"Get some warm water and pour it over."

"Where am I gonna get some warm water?"

My mother always kept a stewpot of warm water on the stove-
top. It wasn't for drinking; it was to create humidity. Coming
from the West Coast, she had trouble adjusting to the dryness of
Fort Vermilion winters. Several times a day, and once before
going to bed, she'd pack the stewpot with snow and leave it on
top of the wood stove to steam up. (She still does this today, only
now she turns the burner on the electric stove to the lowest possible heat and puts a kettle full of tap water on before she turns in
for the night. I tried giving her a humidifier, but it sits unused in
her closet.)

"Go to my place, Lloyd. My mom will give you some water."

"Okay."

And he was off, flying across the field. He was running so fast,
and the sky was getting so dark, that it was mere seconds before
he vanished completely. I was left all alone. My hand, which had
grown numb on the first frozen contact with the steel, began to
hurt. It felt as if I'd fallen into a patch of stinging nettles. I was
crying so hard by now that my nose was running and tears were
soaking into my scarf. All that fluid was freezing into a solid
crust. How long would it take Lloyd Loonskin to run the mile or
so to my house and back again? He was supposed to be quick, but
he seemed to be taking forever. I was seriously considering
pulling my hand away, ripping it off fast like a bandage, when I

spotted him racing back out of the night to save me. He was running full tilt, legs churning through the snow, arms pumping—wait a minute, arms pumping?

"You dummy. You didn't bring any water back?"

I was so mad I took a swing at Lloyd with my free hand. It was ineffectual, but it made me feel better. I wasn't scared any more, I was angry. Talk about being let down.

"I'm sorry, partner."

"Don't say sorry, you dummy."

Calling Lloyd Loonskin a dummy was the greatest insult I could come up with. I knew it would hurt his feelings, but I didn't care.

"I never even went to your place," he said.

"Well, where have you been all this time?"

"I only been gone a few minutes. Just wait up, okay? Think it through. If I go to your house and tell your mom I need some warm water, she's going to want to know what for, and then she's going to ask me where you are, and what am I going to say to that?"

It made perfect sense. And I was furious I hadn't thought about that myself. The whole reason to pour warm water on my hand was to keep my mother from getting mad at me. He was right and I was wrong, but I didn't feel like letting him off the hook that easily.

"You couldn't have come up with a story?" And I added, to be mean, "You dummy."

"You know I can't lie to your mom."

And there it was. He wasn't incapable of telling a lie, the way Bud Peyen was, but he could not and would not tell my mother anything but the absolute truth.

"Don't worry, partner, I got an idea."

And that's when Lloyd Loonskin peed on my hand.

Well, first he had to climb halfway up the post, and then he had to hang on with one gloved hand, and then he peed on my hand. He didn't bother explaining his solution to me first, and that was probably for the best; I might have chosen instead to leave a layer of skin behind on the post, and that would have been painful. Lloyd's solution wasn't painful, but it sure was embarrassing.

The thing was, it worked. The cold metal that had grabbed onto my right hand released its hold, and I was able to pull away without too much damage. My fingers had turned waxy, and they were a disturbing tobacco colour. I couldn't feel anything. There was a deep blue line running at an angle from my index finger onto my palm, where the rough edge of a welded seam had pressed itself deep into my hand, but that didn't seem like anything to worry about. I retrieved my woollen mitt and set about warming my hand back up.

The nerves would spark with pain when my hand finally started thawing out, and the damage from the frostbite, although minor, would be permanent. My right hand still tingles and goes numb with the slightest drop in temperature, and I have the remnants of a thin scar running across my finger and into my palm. Mind you, I had no way of knowing this at the time. At the time, I was just happy there wasn't any blood. I didn't want to get my mother upset.

Lloyd Loonskin and I headed back across the snow to my house. I was still angry about the solution he'd come up with, and it didn't help matters when he started laughing. Then it occurred to me he wasn't going to tell anybody about me freezing my hand or crying, because he wouldn't want me to tell people what he'd done to rescue me. Once I'd figured that out, I started laughing, too. We were laughing so hard we kept falling down, collapsing into the snow, and this would make us laugh even harder. We would pull each other over backwards trying to get up, and that would make us laugh until it hurt.

"I can't believe you peed on my hand."

"Hey, we're partners, right?"

When we finally got to my house, we both went inside to warm up. My mother made us some tea. I soaked my hand in the pot of warm water on the stove. My mother didn't ask why I was doing this, although she must have known something was up because Lloyd Loonskin and I kept bursting into laughter every time we looked at each other. Every time my mother asked us what was so funny, we'd start laughing again. Forget blood brothers. Getting your hand soaked with pee was the true test of friendship.

Lloyd Loonskin and I had met for the first time on our first day of school. It was fifteen minutes before the nine o'clock bell, and I was surrounded by a group of Indian kids who were discussing whether to beat me up before classes started, wait until lunchtime, or do it after school when, presumably, they'd have fewer time constraints. They kept shoving me to the ground while they tried to arrive at a consensus. I wasn't fighting back. I was outnumbered. And I was scared. I didn't want to burst into tears. I knew that wouldn't be good.

"You think you're smart, you," Ted Carrier said. The Carriers lived next door to us, but this was the first time he'd ever said anything to me.

"No," I said, "I'm not smart." I tried to get up, but I was pushed back down.

"Sure, you got a big head, you." That was Junior Ward, who was already in the second grade and a good three years older. He coined the nickname "Big Head," a pejorative that would stay with me throughout my school years. It had nothing to do with being stuck-up or intelligent; I really do have an enormous head, completely out of proportion with the rest of my body. So you have to give him credit for being observant.

"My head isn't big," I said. This time a punch sent me back onto the ground.

"You sure think you're smart, eh?" I had no idea who'd repeated this, but I was at least smart enough to recognize the question as rhetorical.

Fort Vermilion had a fairly rigid, though unwritten, system of class distinction. The Indians considered themselves to be above the half-breeds and both groups looked down on anyone who claimed to be Metis. Bud Peyen once said, in reference to a certain member of the Lizotte family, "He'd lose all his French blood if he cut his finger." Nobody gave the Mennonites much thought. The rest of the white people tended to work for the government or the regular school district or some other symbol of authority. They lived in houses that had power, and most of them had indoor plumbing. They came from out, and they either went back where they'd come from as quickly as they could or gave up and settled in.

The white population of Fort Vermilion lived in three separate enclaves: "the suburbs," up the hill from the Hudson's Bay store and Stephen's General Store; on top of the hill, in school district teacherages; or on the road leading out of town, at the Experimental Farm compound. If an Indian kid or a half-breed kid beat up a white kid, there were usually consequences. My family though, was an anomaly. We were white, but we lived right in town. We lived in a house that had no electricity and no plumbing. We were poor. We were fair game.

My brother Dan had already gone through this. Despite his close friendship with Lucy Noskiye, he wasn't exactly a popular kid. He was big, though, large for his age, and while he wasn't much of a fighter, his size made him difficult to knock down. That was one thing you could say about my brother: he could sure take a punch. By the time I started school, Dan was more or less being left alone. Which suited him fine, since he preferred solitude to the company of other people. I, however, wanted to make friends. I wanted to be popular. Having been saved by the bell that morning, I ran home as fast as possible at lunch. I arrived out of breath, but untouched and unharmed.

"So," my mother asked, "how is your first day at school going?"

"Nobody likes me," I said. And I burst into tears.

My mother was making soup, and by the time she got me to stop crying, the soup was overcooked. Not ruined, but definitely a little burnt. She was still trying to get me to tell her what was wrong when my father arrived.

"Hey, how's school?" That was to me. "What's wrong with the soup?" That was to my mother. My father had lifted the lid off the soup pot to take a sniff and had noticed the smoky smell of burnt vegetables.

My mother took my father into the other room to explain that something traumatic had happened, a situation that would require the very best of their parenting skills. My brother Dan came into the kitchen through the back door.

"You made good time," he said. "What's that smell?" He meant the soup.

"I ran all the way home," I said.

"Oh, yeah." He wasn't too interested.

"They're going to beat me up after school," I said.

"Yeah," he said, "that happens." And then, "Don't tell Mom and Dad."

"Why not?"

"It gets them upset." Dan was setting the table, so I barely heard the next part. "And there's nothing they can do about it, anyways."

My parents came back into the kitchen, united in their desire to comfort me, and they said the right things. I was going to make friends, lots of friends, but it wouldn't happen right away. The rest of the kids at school were as scared as I was. I would be fine, as long as I soldiered on. I felt kind of sorry for them, because they didn't understand the way the world really worked, but I didn't say anything. I nodded and let my mother wipe my nose. Then we all ate the soup. It didn't taste too bad.

The first day of school ended, and I was running home, full tilt, when the ground suddenly jumped up and slapped me in the face. I had been tackled by one of the Mitchell brothers, Willie or Warren or Walter; I wasn't sure, because they all looked alike. Also, they had grabbed me from behind. It didn't matter, anyway, because I was quickly covered by almost the entire grade one class, all of whom started pummelling and kicking me. This recreational activity was called "piling on." How it worked was, one kid would yell out, "Let's pile on so-and-so," and everybody else would participate in a group beating. You could make it stop only by saying you quit or by starting to cry. Both were considered satisfactory endings.

Unwritten rules are the easiest ones to break. I had no idea about the etiquette involved in getting everybody to stop hitting me, but I was bound and determined not to start crying. I already felt like a baby for bursting into tears in front of my mother, and here I was, six years old already, in school. It was time to behave like a grownup. I didn't start crying and I didn't beg them to stop. Instead, I fought back. This wasn't a good decision.

My legs were kicking and my arms were flailing about. I was yelling and shouting and trying to stand up. I don't think I actually made contact with anybody, but the kids did stop punching me. In fact, everybody climbed off me and stepped back. As I slowly got to my feet, I realized I was once again in the epicentre of a circle of Indians. I hoped for a moment that my act of bravery would gain me my freedom, make me part of the gang. It took one quick look around for me to realize neither of these things was going to happen. All I had done, it seemed, was make them mad.

"You think you're tough, eh?"

It was Ted Carrier asking the question, and he didn't give me an opportunity to respond. He punched me in the face, hard. Hard enough to make me stumble and almost fall down again. Hard enough to make my mouth bleed. I was pretty sure that faces were off-limits during pile-ons, but Ted Carrier had escalated the hostilities, and I didn't see any way out of my situation. He punched me again, in the face, and this time I went down on my hands and knees. Then he kicked me in the side of the head.

"Hey, stop it." I couldn't tell who was speaking, but there was a general murmuring and muttering going on in the crowd. I looked up to see who was coming to my defence, and that's when I saw Lloyd Loonskin for the first time.

"None of your business." Ted Carrier wasn't backing down.

"Sure it is," said Lloyd Loonskin. "You can't kick somebody." He shook his head. "That's cowardly."

"Yeah, well, you're cheeky and black, you." That was a big insult, since Lloyd Loonskin was Cree and Ted Carrier was Metis. The full expression was "cheeky and black like a Slavee," since they were darker-skinned. Lloyd Loonskin got an odd look on his face, not angry so much as contemplative. Ted Carrier mistook that look for weakness.

"And," Ted said to Lloyd, "you got no mom."

It was apparently an open secret that Lloyd Loonskin was more or less an orphan and that he lived with his grandmother. Not having a father was nothing to be ashamed of, but not having a mother was unusual. Most kids at least had a mother. It was a cheap shot, especially considering the way Lloyd Loonskin's mother had died, and it wasn't the smartest thing Ted Carrier could have said, not that he would prove to be a Rhodes scholar, anyway.

"Wuff," said Ted Carrier.

Lloyd Loonskin had punched Ted Carrier in the stomach so hard he doubled over and hit his face on the ground.

"Let's pile on Lloyd Loonskin," said Warren Mitchell. "Wuff," he added a second later.

Lloyd Loonskin was two for two. Warren Mitchell was trying to catch his breath, and Ted Carrier had started crying. It was a beautiful sight.

"You want me to hold him for you?" Lloyd Loonskin was offering me the chance to punch Ted Carrier. I took my time crafting an answer.

"No," I said finally, "look at him. He's just a little crybaby."

And everybody laughed. They all started laughing at Ted Carrier. Probably I should have taken Lloyd Loonskin up on his offer, given Ted a good punch, and then I wouldn't have ended up making myself a mortal enemy that day. But that's hindsight.

My younger brother Sean had been putting up a fuss that afternoon. My mother had him on her lap, bouncing him up and down gently and singing to him in a quiet voice. She almost dropped him when the front door banged open and in I came, my jacket torn and dirty, my mouth bloody, my left eye already starting to swell up. I had someone with me.

"This is Lloyd Loonskin," I said, with the biggest, bloodiest smile you could imagine. "He's my best friend."

And so we were. And that was even before we found out we'd been born on more or less the same day.

Nineteen sixty-seven, the year it snowed, in July, was also the year Lloyd Loonskin got lost in the woods. It was my fault, sort of. It was September, and Lloyd and I had decided to go exploring. There was an abandoned trapper's shack somewhere north of the Hilltop Mission, way out in the woods, and we decided to find it. Lloyd claimed he knew where it was, but we fought our way through the bush for hours with no success. We weren't wearing proper jackets, and although the mosquitoes were done for the season, there were still plenty of black flies about. We were getting chewed up. And the sun was starting to go down. We had stopped talking to each other some time earlier, so when we stepped out of the trees and onto a gravel road, neither of us said anything for a long time.

"We've been going in circles." I was the first to break the silence.

"No, we weren't."

"This is the road to La Crete."

"No, it's not."

"Yeah, it is." I was irritated. "You can see the top of the power lines over there by the bend. We go down to the corner and then we head south and we're back in town."

"We haven't found the cabin."

"At least we're not lost."

"We haven't seen anything interesting," he said. "What's the point?"

"Well, whose fault is that?" I wasn't interested in continuing our adventure. I was happy we were so close to civilization, and I wanted to get home for supper. "You're the one who said you could find this cabin, and instead you got us lost in the woods."

"You just said we're not lost."

"Well, not now."

"So?"

"So what?"

"So, are you coming with me or what?"

"Are you crazy?" I couldn't believe he was being this stubborn. "Forget about it. We'll go find that stupid old cabin some other time."

"I'm not giving up." He seemed stuck on his plan, but I probably could still have talked him into coming back to my place.

My mother was making stew. Lloyd Loonskin really liked my mother's stew. The problem was, he wouldn't leave things alone.

"Maybe you're scared," said Lloyd Loonskin, "but I'm not, me."

And that was that. "I'm not scared," I said.

"You're scared, you."

"You don't know where this cabin is. You'll get lost, and then you'll be *plenty* scared."

"I'm going."

"Don't be so stupid . . . " It was out of my mouth before I could take it back. Lloyd Loonskin was sensitive on the subject of his intelligence. Calling him a dummy was bad enough, but "stupid" was particularly hurtful. I tried to take the sting out of it. "Jeez, I don't mean you're stupid. I mean it's a stupid idea."

He didn't say anything; he simply turned and headed back to the woods. He stopped at the edge and turned around.

"So," he said, "you're not coming?"

"I don't think so."

"Okay, I'll see you later."

He stepped into the woods, and I waited until he was out of earshot before muttering "you dummy" to myself. I went home, figuring he'd find his way back to his grandmother's on his own. I thought he was showing off. He wasn't really going to look for the cabin; he was going to go home. What a dummy.

Lloyd Loonskin didn't show up at his grandmother's house that night. She waited for him until almost nine o'clock. Then she made the long walk up the hill to see if he was still at my house. She knew we were friends. She didn't speak any English, and my father went over and got our neighbour Violet Moberly to come and translate. I didn't say anything to Lloyd's grandmother about having an argument with him. I just said the last time I'd seen him he was heading into the woods.

Corporal Ledinski took charge of the situation. He was the law in Fort Vermilion. Word went through town quickly, and anybody with bush sense showed up at the RCMP building that night. They started looking for Lloyd Loonskin first thing next morning. I couldn't sleep. It felt like my fault Lloyd Loonskin was lost. It made me sick to think about it. The nights were getting colder; you could see your breath after the sun went down. The kids at school would talk about which fathers had gone out into the woods, but nobody ever mentioned Lloyd. It was as if they were afraid to say his name.

More and more men left their houses and joined the search. They stayed out in the bush; none of them wanted to come back until somebody had found him. After three days of waiting and worrying, there was still no sign of Lloyd Loonskin, and the search parties were being expanded.

"Get your gun, Hank." That was Donny Paul; he had shown up early in the morning with Bud Peyen. My father was being drafted into service.

"He's been out there for three days," my father said.

"We're still looking for him, Hank," said Bud Peyen. "We're gonna keep looking until we find him."

Donny Paul explained the rules.

"If you find him, fire three shots into the air and we'll all come running fast."

"If he's alive," my father said.

"Sure."

"What if he's dead?"

"Then fire one shot," Donny Paul said. "We'll come and get you, but we won't rush."

My father had one more question, and he knew it was going to be awkward. He waited until Donny Paul had left.

"Bud," he said, "do you have an extra rifle?"

"You don't have a gun?"

"Well, no."

"Do you have a deck of cards?"

"Yes," said my father.

"Take them with you," Bud Peyen said. "If you get lost you can sit down and start playing solitaire."

"How does that help?"

"Well," said Bud Peyen, "you know how it is . . . sooner or later somebody's going to tap you on the shoulder and tell you that the red jack goes on the black queen."

This made my father smile, and Bud Peyen put his arm around my father as they went out the door. Bud Peyen knew the woods could kill you. After three days of searching, it was pretty well accepted that Lloyd Loonskin wasn't coming home.

Sixtoes Mitchell wasn't called Sixtoes because he had an extra digit on one foot, or because he'd lost four toes to frostbite, or anything like that. Sixtoes was his given name. Nobody knew how his parents came up with it. Sixtoes Mitchell was a legendary figure among the local trappers and hunters. Not only because his trapline brought in more furs every winter than the next three combined, and not only because he was generally considered to be the finest shot in the area, but also because he was, quite simply, the scariest-looking man in the world. He looked, Bud Peyen said, as if his face had caught on fire and they'd put it out with an axe. All of us kids considered Sixtoes Mitchell to be the most frightening grownup around. He never seemed to speak, and he always looked as if he was going to hurt someone. If anyone was going to track down Lloyd Loonskin, it was Sixtoes Mitchell.

Lloyd Loonskin had spent four nights in the woods, and he was well and truly lost. But it was probably a good thing that his grandmother had raised him, because he had enough bush sense even at seven years of age to keep himself alive. He knew enough to pull his jean jacket up over his shoulders and button it around his head so he wouldn't lose heat. He knew how to twist spruce branches into a bed. He knew how to pull cattails up and get the juice out of them when he got hungry. And, most important, he knew to follow the direction the water was going, because that would eventually take him to the Peace River and he would find his way home by following the riverbank. The problem was, Lloyd got so hungry and so thirsty around the second day he became disoriented. By the third day, he finally got too tired to walk, so he built himself a little shelter under a Jack pine. He hadn't given up, but he was getting worried. He had tried several times to start a fire, but he wasn't able to get one going. He decided to lie down and have a nap. He knew you weren't supposed to go to sleep in the woods when you were really cold and really hungry, but he figured if he could rest for a bit he'd be able to figure out what to do next.

By his fifth morning out in the bush, Lloyd knew he was in serious trouble. He couldn't stop shaking. His whole body was vibrating, and he felt as if he had a fever. He was so thirsty his throat was closing up, and, to top everything off, it sounded as if an animal was coming close to the little lean-to he had built. It sounded like a large animal, could even be a bear, and Lloyd was already thinking that he wasn't going to see his grandmother ever again when he took a peek through the branches. It was worse than he could have imagined. Sixtoes Mitchell, the most terrifying man in the world, seemed to be coming straight towards him. Carrying a rifle. Lloyd Loonskin decided the only thing to do was stay completely still. He figured he was hidden well enough that Sixtoes Mitchell wouldn't see him, as long as he could keep himself from shaking.

My father and Bud Peyen were also in the woods. They were walking a circle-8 route, staying within shouting distance and joining up to eat and compare notes. My father hated to admit it, even to himself, but he was having a good time. It was a terrible thing, with Lloyd Loonskin who knows where, but the whole experience, sleeping out in the bush, eating bannock and lard, even learning a little tracking technique . . . well, there was something exhilarating about it. It was fun, was what my father was thinking, and who better to share it with than his friend Bud Peyen. He was about to say something along these lines to Bud when the silence was shattered by a single rifle shot.

There was a moment of indescribable tension as both men waited for the second and third gunshots. Two seconds went by, then three, then four, and still nothing. My father turned to say something to Bud Peyen, but the big man sat down suddenly, collapsing onto the ground. He was weeping, the tears pouring out of his eyes. It astonished my father, and he couldn't think of anything else to do, so he knelt next to Bud Peyen, put his arms around him, and let him cry. It was so sad it made my father feel as if the world had ended.

Back at the lean-to, Lloyd Loonskin was so frightened at seeing Sixtoes Mitchell that he'd decided to run for his life. Sixtoes got the first shot off, then went crashing through the bush after Lloyd. Despite his weak condition, Lloyd was so terrified that catching him was a little difficult. Sixtoes finally grabbed him, threw him to the ground, put a foot on his back to hold him there, and fired the next two shots. Lloyd Loonskin had been lost in the woods for five nights and six days.

Sixtoes Mitchell wasn't much of a talker, but he was persuaded to tell the search party how he had found Lloyd Loonskin. He'd been tracking Lloyd for two full days, but he could tell from the signs he picked up on that the boy was growing weak. His footprints were meandering, directionless, and he was stopping to rest far too often. Sixtoes was worried he wouldn't find Lloyd

Loonskin in time. When he spotted the crudely constructed lean-to and saw something moving inside, he smiled to himself and cocked his rifle.

"That's when the boy up and ran," said Sixtoes Mitchell.

"You scared him," Bud Peyen said. "You don't smile that often, and when you do it's like your face splits in half."

Lloyd was returned to his grandmother after one night in the hospital. He was dehydrated and suffering from exposure to the elements, but it didn't take him long to bounce back. The town threw a party. They called it Lloyd Loonskin Day. The Catholic priest, Father Litzler, the Protestant minister, Reverend McTeague, and a Mennonite lay preacher from the Hilltop Mission named Ben DeVeer gave the first ecumenical service in the town's history. Corporal Ledinski, in his dress reds, made a speech praising Sixtoes Mitchell, who had to be practically dragged up onstage, and who looked very scary when he got there. My father read a poem by Robert Frost about a road in the woods. Narcisse Lizotte played the fiddle. Edward Carrier played his guitar. Bud Peyen played his drum and sang a traditional song. In the middle of it all, in his best white shirt and a pair of black pants, was Lloyd Loonskin. He was wearing a sash that Thelma Two Shoes had made for him. It read, "Loyld Loonsin, lost boy came home to us." She was never much on spelling, Thelma, but you couldn't argue with the sentiment.

Afterwards, more drums were brought out and blankets were placed on the cold ground and all the men got down on their knees to do some gambling. The women were dancing, and everybody—white people, Indians, and Metis—was celebrating together. The party went on until dawn, although all of the Mennonites left around midnight. The most interesting thing about it all was that it just happened. Nobody was in charge, and nobody planned anything.

I was sure happy Lloyd Loonskin had made it back. He was getting a lot of attention, and I have to confess that there was a part of me that was jealous. The big dummy gets lost in the woods, and the next thing you know they're throwing him a party. But in the middle of one of the speeches, Lloyd looked down at me and winked. That felt pretty good.

six

PERFECT CRIME

There was a large pile of dirt in our front yard. The dirt was there because my father had finally decided we needed to drill a well. Until then we had been getting our water from Frankie Flett, the Water Man. Nobody called him Frank, or Mr. Flett; he was Frankie Flett, the Water Man, and he was the only provider of water in Fort Vermilion. Unless you lived in a teacherage or at the Experimental Farm, that is; then your water came from the aqueduct system, an apparently random series of leaky pipes. Whoever had installed them didn't seem to know that water is supposed to run downhill, which meant little water pressure and frequent sewer backups. The Romans may have invented plumbing, but the Fort Vermilion system seemed to have been designed by Visigoths.

My father came to his decision to have a well dug after watching Frankie Flett, the Water Man, load up one day. Frankie Flett, the Water Man, had a flatbed wagon, which was pulled by two enormous Clydesdales. The one with the white patch on its face was called Daisy, even though the patch of hair looked exactly like a five-point star. We all thought Star would have been a better name. The other horse was called simply "Horse," because Frankie Flett, the Water Man, had never bothered to name it. We figured it deserved a name of some kind, so all the kids in town called it Clyde.

The team was well taken care of, and they were an impressive sight. The Clydesdales were by far the largest animals in the area. Domesticated, that is. A full-grown bull moose would probably have come close in size, and the bison that occasionally wandered up from Wood Buffalo National Park were larger, but you didn't see them pulling carts or ploughing fields or otherwise doing an honest day's work. The wagon the horses pulled had room for twelve water barrels. These were old oil drums that had been cleaned out. Before the roads to Fort Vermilion were improved, before tanker trucks could safely make the trip year-round, diesel fuel and gas were delivered to our area in fifty-gallon metal casks. Once these were emptied, they were up for grabs, and everybody had one sitting outside their house, for collecting the rain and for Frankie Flett, the Water Man, to fill up. You made sure they were clean by burning off the insides, then scrubbing them out with lye. They may not have been the most sanitary receptacles for drinking water, but they worked fine.

Frankie Flett, the Water Man, would show up at our house on a regular basis. He would back his team up and then use a five-gallon pail to empty out one of his water barrels into ours. He didn't keep to a particular schedule; he seemed to know when your water supply was getting low, and he'd stop by to replenish it. He charged fifty cents a barrel on delivery, and he didn't extend credit. Forty-five gallons of water would last a couple of weeks, depending on how much cooking was being done, how many kettles were being boiled for tea, and how many baths were being taken. Our family bathed every Sunday night, boiling the water on the stove and then filling a deep square sheet-metal tub that would be wrestled in from the yard. There were now six of us in the family—my youngest brother Billy had been born three years earlier—and baths were taken youngest to oldest, which meant my mother and father spent those years washing in tepid grey water. We also had a sponge bath every morning. That was face, ears, armpits and feet. My brothers and I weren't too fond of the weekly hot-water cleaning, but the morning cleaning was worse, because the water was cold. Frankie Flett, the Water Man, considered us good customers, since we used way more water than most of the people in town. Many families bathed on a less-frequent schedule. Fifty cents was a lot of money.

Frankie Flett, the Water Man, filled his barrels in the Peace River. There was a trail down to the river by the Factor's House that the Hudson's Bay Company had built back in the 1930s. When water and power became available in the early 1950s, the Hudson's Bay had built a new house for their store manager and abandoned the old one. It had sat empty since then, but no one had ever broken into it or vandalized it in any manner. The windows still had all the original glass, and a tree branch snapping off and landing on the back porch had caused the only damage.

My father had noticed Frankie Flett, the Water Man, taking his wagon down the hill to the river one afternoon. He was glad to see him, since he wanted to arrange for an earlier delivery. An outbreak of head lice in the community had my father concerned, and he planned to increase the frequency with which our family bathed. He had also picked up some medicinal shampoo that was supposed to prevent lice, and the instructions on the bottle said to use fresh water with each application. This all meant using extra water, and that was why my father followed Frankie Flett, the

Water Man, down the hill, and saw for the first time the process he used when filling up his wagon.

"He walks the horses right into the river," my father said, "and he loads the water from the back of the wagon."

"Yeah, okay," said Bud Peyen.

Bud Peyen had been invited for dinner that night. As he always did when he was invited to stay, he had gone into the kitchen to count the servings. The first time he did this my mother was perplexed, but she figured it out quickly. People were poor in Fort Vermilion. They were used to being poor, and traditions had developed out of this long-term poverty. If someone was offering a meal, you went and counted the pork chops before accepting to make sure you weren't eating food that was meant for somebody else. It was crucial to make sure children got enough to eat. It was considered a huge breach of etiquette to take food meant to feed a kid. As we would learn that evening, Sparky Caldwell had found this out the hard way.

Sparky was a large, gregarious Mormon who had arrived in Fort Vermilion to work as a laboratory and x-ray technician at the hospital. He had curly red hair and a round, freckled red face. He was heavy, like many of the men in town, but without the muscle tone underneath we were used to seeing. Sparky was soft-looking, given to huffing and puffing if he had to do anything physical. His wife was as thin as he was fat, and their children took after one or the other of them, being either thin and dark or soft and pink. His real name wasn't Sparky, of course, his real name was Steve, but he made sure everyone knew his preference.

"Call me Sparky," he said. "Everybody does."

If you have to give yourself your own nickname, there is probably something wrong with you at a deep-seated level, but that wasn't the reason nobody liked Sparky. What had happened, Bud told us, was this. Having an interest in all things aboriginal,

Sparky had invited some of the local Indians over to his house for a meal. This wasn't done randomly. He had invited Thelma Carrier, who worked at the hospital with him, and she had brought her husband, Cliff. Bud Peyen had done some landscaping for the Caldwell family, so Sparky had invited Bud over as well, and Bud had brought along Yvette Mercredi, who he was sweet on and trying to impress.

The meal was tasty, but the evening wasn't a success. It wasn't because Sparky Caldwell kept trying to turn the dinner-table conversation into a discussion of the lost tribe of Israel and the cultural differences among local tribes. The Indians in Fort Vermilion were used to odd behaviour from white people, and strained and awkward conversations with them were the rule, not the exception. So that wasn't the problem. The electric stove that was used to cook the meal impressed Yvette Mercredi, and Bud Peyen found the fact that Mormons didn't drink coffee interesting. Bud wasn't much on drinking coffee himself, but he was confused when he found out Mormons didn't drink tea, either. He wondered how they got up in the morning, and he figured the lack of tea-drinking was likely responsible for Sparky Caldwell's flabby physique and general poor health. He didn't say anything, of course; he didn't want to appear impolite.

But when the meal was finished, and the pie about to come out, Sparky Caldwell did something so completely unacceptable that it would become the talk of the town for months. Among the Indians, at any rate. Sparky's youngest daughter hadn't finished her glass of milk, and Sparky reached over, picked up her glass, and drank the contents.

Lots of parents have done this, of course, in the interests of being thrifty. What are you going to do? Put the milk back in the fridge? Pour it down the sink? Might as well finish it off. But this action was perceived rather differently in Fort Vermilion. Among the Indians, at any rate. First of all, this wasn't powdered milk, like most of us drank; this was real milk that came in a glass bottle from the dairy. You could pay a premium for real milk at Stephen's General Store, whenever they managed to bring in a shipment, or you could drive over to High Level to pick some up. Either way, it was an expensive and time-consuming matter to put real milk on the table. You could buy unpasteurized milk from the Mennonites for cheaper, but that still meant a road trip to La Crete. The *kind* of milk Sparky drank, though, was not the issue. The issue was taking milk from your own child, and the gaffe would cost Sparky Caldwell big-time.

Sparky was putting the empty glass down when Thelma Carrier looked over at Bud Peyen. Her eyes were wide with disbelief. Yvette Mercredi, normally a cheerful and fun-loving girl, had compressed her lips into a thin line, a look of monumental disapproval on her face. Sparky Caldwell noticed the sudden shift in mood, but he couldn't figure out what had happened. His normally ruddy face became redder than ever, and he started to sweat profusely.

"Thanks for having us over," said Bud Peyen.

It was like a dam bursting. All the Indians got up to put on their coats and their boots. They were absolutely silent, and they were very quick to get dressed.

"Aren't you going to stay?" That was Sparky Caldwell, adding, hopelessly, "There's pie."

"I guess we're not hungry," Bud Peyen said, and he was almost out the door when he said it, leaving a confused group of Mormons with a mess of pie to eat on their own.

"I should have said, what's the point in eating pie if you can't wash it down with some tea?" This was Bud again, but now he was telling my father the story, and the rest of us were listening in. "What sort of person does that?"

"Well, Bud, they don't drink any alcohol, either."

Bud Peyen didn't understand the connection.

"They're Mormons," my father said. "No stimulants of any kind."

"I meant what kind of man would take the milk from his own child," said Bud Peyen. "I wish I could have thought of something to say to him, but I was so shocked."

Now it was my father's turn to understand.

"Well, Bud, it's not like he pulled his joint out of his trousers and slapped it down on the table."

"Hank," said Bud Peyen, "it was worse than that."

My father didn't argue the point. He knew the town had turned on Sparky Caldwell, and now he knew the reason why. Unwritten rules, again. The Caldwell family were already making plans to return to southern Alberta, where they would be back among their own kind. There were plenty of Mormons around Cardston and Claresholm and such. The shunning had affected them deeply, and they were now home-schooling their kids. Not because the kids were getting beaten up at school or anything, but because they were being completely ignored. Worst of all, nobody would call Sparky by his nickname. He became "Mr. Caldwell," delivered in the coldest of tones, for the rest of his time in Fort Vermilion. My mother felt sorry for Sparky, though. She had an outsider's perspective on how hard it was to be accepted in Fort Vermilion.

"I don't think he meant anything by it," she said.

"Look," said Bud Peyen, "he took the milk away from his daughter and he drank it."

And that was that. The mystery was solved. My father wanted to change the subject back to Frankie Flett, the Water Man.

"Bud, he takes his team right into the river."

"Yeah, okay."

"That means the horses are upstream."

"Sure."

"Bud, he's getting the water downstream of where the horses are."

"Yeah, okay," said Bud Peyen. "I think everybody knows that, Hank."

"Bud, I'm going to hook up to the town water."

"If you think that's a good idea."

"All right, I'm asking you what *you* think."

"Because the town water comes from the reservoir."

The town water supply came from a concrete basin at the top of the hill. There was an old chain-link fence around it, most of which had given in to gravity.

"I'm aware of that," said my father.

"They pump that water right up out of the Peace River."

My father could tell Bud Peyen was working his way around to telling him something.

"They use a big diesel pump," said Bud Peyen. "It's pretty loud."

My father didn't say anything. He'd learned from experience that when Bud Peyen was working his way around to saying something, questions threw him off track.

"It's the same exact water Frankie Flett, the Water Man, brings you."

"Without the horse added," my father said, hoping this wouldn't derail Bud Peyen.

"You ever thought about putting in a well?"

"Now why would I want to do that?"

"The town water comes from the reservoir."

Bud Peyen was starting to repeat himself. This meant he was finally leading up to something important. My father waited, silently, for the penny to drop.

"You know Ted Cardinal, him?"

"The little wiry guy with no teeth?"

"No, that's his brother, Tim."

"The tall skinny guy with the broken nose?"

"No, that's his cousin, Tom."

"The one with the funny eye?"

"That's the one."

"Well," said my father, "what about him?"

"He works for the town, eh?"

"Okay."

"He came by my place, him."

"Right."

"Anyway," said Bud Peyen, "me and Ted Cardinal?"

"Yes?"

"Last week we pulled a dead cow out of that reservoir."

My father was progressing nicely in teaching Bud Peyen how to read and write. A few weeks later, when he was trying to teach Bud the meaning of the word "appalled," he told him to remember the look my father had had on his face when Bud mentioned the dead cow in the town's water supply.

"We figured it would be better, maybe, not to tell the white people," Bud said helpfully.

"That was probably the right decision," my father agreed.

So—a well it would be. To get the work under way, my father hired the Carruthers twins: Left-handed Frank Carruthers and his right-handed brother, who was also named Frank. The brothers were well regarded for their skill in building wells and their ability to locate water. Even the Mennonites hired them, which was unusual because the Mennonites rarely needed to hire anyone to do anything. The Carruthers found water in our yard and put in a well and dug out enough ground for a septic tank. They also dug a basement directly in front of our house, and Bud Peyen poured the concrete for the floor and built the cinder-block walls. John Wiebe and a team from the Hilltop Mission jacked our house up and rolled it forward onto the new foundation. Donald Banks came in to finish off the plumbing. After nine years of living in Fort Vermilion, we finally had an indoor toilet. We celebrated with a ceremonial bonfire: we poured kerosene into the outhouse and threw a lit match in after it. As we watched the building blaze away, my father was inspired to gather his sons around him.

"Boys," he told us, "always remember. It's easy to burn down the outhouse; the hard part is putting in new plumbing."

Oh, but it was heaven. No more frigid trips to the bathroom in the middle of winter. No more using a candle to warm the seat. We still didn't have hot water; the upgrades had cost a fortune, and my father decided to wait on putting in the electric.

This was maybe the happiest time we ever had as a family. Watching the outhouse burn to the ground. Turning the taps on and off and on and off again. Flushing the toilet and watching the water spiral away. My mother with her arm around my father, smiling up at him, her eyes sparkling, his eyes twinkling. Even when they yelled at us to stop fooling around with the taps and leave the toilet alone, you could tell they weren't really angry. We kids couldn't hold it in. We *had* to shout and yell and run around making noise.

My parents had been busy since they'd come to Fort Vermilion, and not just busy turning out children. The place may have felt like a wrong turn at the outset, but they'd made the best of things since their arrival. My mother and father weren't considered locals, not yet, but they were beginning to fit in.

It wasn't long after they'd moved into town that they got invited to their first Tea Dance. They had heard drumming almost every night, and they were curious. My father consulted the one person who might be able to provide a satisfactory explanation.

"It's a Tea Dance, Hank," said Bud Peyen. "That's what we call it."

"Fascinating," my father said. "Why do you call it that?"

"Well, we all drink tea," Bud Peyen said. "And then we dance."

The Tea Dance was also called the Round Dance. It was traditional to throw one whenever you wanted to celebrate. The rules and etiquette were very complicated. Bud Peyen tried to describe how a Tea Dance worked, but my father was having trouble understanding.

"You can't learn about a Tea Dance from talking," said Bud. "The next Tea Dance, I'll come get you and Louise and the boys and we'll go."

"Is it all right?" my mother asked. "Are we allowed to attend?"

"Sure," said Bud Peyen. "We don't kick anybody out."

A good Tea Dance could last for several days, and nobody ever seemed to get tired of dancing. We didn't realize it at the time, but one of the functions of a Tea Dance was to stop people from leaving home and never coming back.

The residential school had closed during the years my parents had been in Fort Vermilion, and Indian kids were allowed in the public school after 1963. My mother helped start up a library board in town, and my father was the scoutmaster for the most northerly Boy Scout troop in the world. The scoutmaster thing came about following an argument my father had with his boss, Gene Rogers.

Gene Rogers ran the Junior Forest Wardens, a program that provided activities for boys from ages six to sixteen. They went on canoe trips and camped out overnight. They wore spiffy red shirts and fake Mountie hats. It looked like fun, but my father wouldn't let us join up. He was trying to get Gene Rogers to allow Indian kids into the organization.

"As long as I'm running the Junior Forest Wardens, the rules aren't changing." That would be Gene Rogers, who hated my father by this point.

"That's narrow-minded and short-sighted." This would be my father, who didn't care what his boss thought about him. "Gene, you're always complaining about the native students— they're lazy, they've got no initiative, idle hands and all of that. Think about how much good you could do, think about the effect you could have on their lives."

Gene Rogers was actually thinking about how much he wanted to fire my father. "Hank, you might be as sneaky as a Philadelphia lawyer, but you can't find a loophole here. We are not letting Indians join the Junior Forest Wardens. Indians are naturally passive and undisciplined . . . "

That was as far as he got. My father had heard this lecture before, and he had no interest in listening to it again.

"Gene, first of all, you're wrong," said my father, "dead wrong. And even if you were right, which you are not, think of how these children would respond to the teamwork and camaraderie you could provide."

"Hank, if you think they need it so much, why don't you start your own group?"

And so he did. I'm not sure Lord Baden-Powell would have approved of vengeance and retribution as motives for starting a Boy Scout troop, but my father got one up and running, and it became a huge hit. He didn't just follow the rulebook, either; he had Sixtoes Mitchell come in and teach tracking, and Bud Peyen taught traditional drumming. John Wiebe showed the kids some woodworking techniques. They started up a softball team, and my father's Boy Scouts took on Gene Rogers and his Junior Forest Wardens. They cleaned their clocks.

Everybody in town had turned out for the big game, and for weeks afterwards my father couldn't walk anywhere without some Indian coming up to him, looking him in the eye, and nodding. Sometimes the person would shake his hand. I heard him telling my mother about it one afternoon, before she shooed my brothers and me out of the house. "You kids go outside and play," she said, and not in the mildest of tones. "I can't hear myself think in here." She was so relieved to see us go that she forgot to tell us not to play on the pile of dirt in our front yard.

That pile of dirt was almost a mountain. It was an inspirational sight, prompting me to invent a game I called Fall Down the Hill. It worked like this: Lloyd Loonskin and I would lie at the bottom of the hill with sticks for guns. My brothers Sean and Billy would run as fast as they could up the back of the hill. Then, upon hearing me or Lloyd Loonskin yell, "Bang, bang," they would throw themselves off the top of the hill and roll down the dirt until they died at our feet. After that, we'd do it again. Sometimes treats were involved. If we had cupcakes or—and this was rare—candy, I would collect it from my brothers. The one who created the most dramatic death scene would have his piece of cake or chocolate returned to him. I would split the loser's piece with Lloyd Loonskin. If Lloyd hadn't shown up that day, I would get the loser's piece all to myself. Being a big brother was fun.

One day after school let out, while playing a particularly rousing round of Fall Down the Hill, I came up with a good idea. It grew out of a conversation Lloyd Loonskin and I were having during the down times, when my younger brothers were climbing the back of the hill.

"We should break into the school."

"Yeah, that would be fun."

"Climb in through a window."

"Yeah, except they lock them all."

"Except that one in the furnace room."

"Yeah, they never lock that one."

"That's 'cause it's too small. You couldn't climb through."

It doesn't matter which one of us was saying what. We were engaging in an idle intellectual pursuit. If, and this was purely hypothetical, but if we were going to break into the school, how—and again this was pure speculation—would that be managed? We had reached an impasse and would probably have changed the subject, except that my brother Sean appeared on the crest of the hill and caused the entire plan to spring to life in my head. Sean was only six. He was tiny. He was small enough to fit through the window. All we'd have to do was shove him through and let him fall eight or nine feet to the concrete floor. Then, if he hadn't broken anything, he would come around to the door and let us in. Once we were inside we'd be able to, well, we hadn't thought that part through. We weren't the most seasoned of criminals. But it was the perfect plan. I was a genius.

The plan went awry almost immediately. First of all, my brother Billy wasn't pleased that he would be left behind, and he put up such a fuss that we had to take him with us. Then my brother Sean got moody about being the one doing the actual breaking in and had to be threatened. He kept asking why we wanted to break into the school, and what we were going to do once we got in there. His negative outlook would have earned him a punch, but we needed him for the plan to work. What was with all these questions? What were we going to do? Well, we were going to take stuff. Or do stuff. We'd be in the school. We'd think of something.

It never occurred to me that teachers, like students, do homework. And even if it had, I would certainly never have thought that teachers, unlike students, would do their homework in the school after hours. But my brother Sean made so much noise landing in the furnace room that he attracted the immediate attention of a teacher who was new to our school that year. She was nice and smart and inspiring, and the reason I can't remember her name is because, like most brand-new educators who got their first employment opportunities in Fort Vermilion, she didn't come back for a second year. Most teachers of quality fled the town as soon as they could get a job closer to civilization. The ones who stayed had either fallen in love with the rugged beauty of the True North or were unable to find work anywhere else because they were incompetent or truly evil. Sometimes they were *both* incompetent and truly evil. Anyway, this nice young teacher taught grade one, which made her Sean's teacher. He adored her, and being caught breaking into your own school by a teacher you adore is bound to be upsetting.

I had almost made it home at a dead run when Lloyd Loonskin caught up to me and dragged me back to the scene of the crime. Lloyd was of the opinion that, having put my brother in this situation, we should go back and face the consequences. I thought he was crazy, but he had a strong grip on my arm, and he wasn't letting go. We'd left my brother Billy behind as well, which Lloyd Loonskin pointed out was more than enough evidence to link me to the break-in attempt. We went back to face the music.

I tried to talk my way out of it. I had some story about needing to get a schoolbook or something along that line. Nobody was buying it, though, not the teacher, not Corporal Ledinski, and, worst of all, not my mother. I was taken downtown to the RCMP building and put in a cell. I was held there for a month, all by myself, with nobody to talk to and no food or water. At least, that's how I remember it. The truth is, I was given an hour or two to think about my crime, and then I was released into the care of my father, who didn't seem as upset about the incident as my mother was. They even had a whispered argument about it after I was sent to bed, she saying his lack of action would encourage me in a life of crime, his defence being somewhere along the lines of "boys will be boys." I was grounded for a month, and I had to tell my younger siblings that I was sorry for putting them in harm's way. They got off scot-free.

Lloyd Loonskin didn't get into any trouble, either. He was released to his grandmother; he didn't even get a lecture. Corporal Ledinski had said that he was disappointed in me and he expected more of me. I figured maybe they didn't expect anything of Lloyd Loonskin, and that was why he wasn't being punished. Lucky guy. Lloyd didn't have to stick around after the break-in. He could have gone home, and nobody would have known he was involved. But no, he had to go and drag me back. What a dummy.

$\mathcal{S}$TANDING
BUFFALO

he summer after my attempted break-in was the same summer that we got two new sisters and a new dog. It was the start of our year Down South, and it looked as if it was going to be a good year at first. It didn't turn out that way, even though I managed to make my film debut, in a nude scene no less.

We had to move because my father got fired. Gene Rogers, tired of my father's insubordination, and of losing at softball, had looked at his original job application and uncovered my father's lack of a proper teaching certificate. The jig was up. Gene Rogers gleefully passed the information on to the school board, and my father was dismissed on the spot. It was the talk of the town. The white people were outraged by my father's deception. The Indians were outraged that he had lost his job. They all thought my father was a fine teacher, and they didn't see what a piece of paper had to do with his abilities in the classroom.

My parents had spent ten years in Fort Vermilion. Three of their four sons had been born there. They owned property, and they had recently fixed up their house. But they had very little money left. Putting in the plumbing had used up almost all their savings. My father needed to find some other way to support his family. He spent a few miserable weeks working on a road crew south of High Level, but he wasn't good at it. He cashed one paycheque and that was that.

Next, he talked Bud Peyen into accompanying him to the Northwest Territories, to see if there were any jobs available in Hay River or Yellowknife. There weren't. Scott Wagner, the Hudson's Bay store manager, had grown tired of lending my father his camera and finally given him one outright. So even though he didn't find work, he did come home with some lovely colour slides of Eskimos. He also got into trouble with Bud Peyen.

He told us all about it once he got back. He and Bud had been on their way back to Fort Vermilion. What little cash they'd picked up doing odd jobs had almost completely run out. My father felt the trip had been a colossal waste of time and money. Bud Peyen thought it was a thrill. He'd never been so far away from home. It was the best time he'd ever had, and he would continue to refer to it often, always describing the trip as "the time me and Hank went prospecting." They'd stopped in Hay River. The only restaurant in town was closed for the day, so they ended up in a bar. My father was still on the wagon then, he'd kept his promise to my mother, and he had long ago quit smoking as well, although that was due more to economic pressures than to willpower. Bud Peyen was never much for alcohol at the best of times. Still, they ended up in this bar, hoping to pick up a quick bite and some tea for Bud Peyen and some coffee for my father.

There were a number of what Bud Peyen always referred to as "city boys" hanging out in a large and rowdy group by the pool table. I guess there was something about an Indian as big as Bud that rubbed them the wrong way. Or maybe it was the fact that he was in the company of my father. It didn't matter. They were young and far away from home, and they were drunk.

"Hey, Chief, give us a dance." That would be asshole number one.

"Yeah, a rain dance, eh?" Asshole number two.

"Hey, Chief, can't you hear us? We're talking to you." Number three.

"Maybe he don't speak any English," said asshole number one. "Hey, Chief, you speak English?"

My father decided it was time to go.

"Bud, forget the food. Let's get back in the car."

"Those boys sure are rude."

"Yeah, I know. Don't let them bother you."

Bud Peyen stepped back from the bar and shambled his way over to the crowd, which was looking more like a mob to my father.

"Excuse me, boys," Bud Peyen said. "Can I ask you something, me?"

There was much laughter at his approach and his mild tone of voice. My father wasn't fooled; he was trying to circle around behind the group, and he was reminding himself to be sure to take off his glasses if anything started.

"See," said Bud, "my friend here and I are having an argument."

This caused every eye to turn and focus on my father. So much for the element of surprise, my father thought.

"He don't think you boys are fit to eat with the pigs," said Bud Peyen.

My father was now receiving the undivided attention of a dangerously silent group. They looked fit and young, and my father couldn't imagine why Bud Peyen wanted to make them mad.

"Yeah," Bud Peyen said, "he don't think you're fit to eat with the pigs," and he lifted asshole number one off the ground with one hand while he continued, "but I say you is."

My father, often given to hyperbole, never tried to exaggerate his part in the brawl. He snatched his glasses off, and in the time it took him to do it he heard several dull, meaty thumps. He put his glasses back on. Asshole number one was curled up on top of the pool table. Assholes two and three were flat out on the floor. Assholes four through nine didn't seem to be behaving in an aggressive manner. My father stepped up beside Bud Peyen.

"You should probably say you're sorry to my friend," he said. "And I want you to know that, of the two of us, he's the gentle one."

This wasn't an outright lie. Of the two of them, it was my father who had the temper. Asshole number one mumbled something that sounded enough like an apology to satisfy Bud Peyen and my father, and they collected their sandwiches and their Thermoses and left.

"You know, Hank," said Bud Peyen as they were climbing into the Zephyr, "them white boys get to drinking and they think they're bulletproof."

When they returned to Fort Vermilion, Bud Peyen dined out for months on his stories. He talked about working alongside Eskimo men who were half his size but just as strong. He talked about riding an elevator to the bottom of the Maple Mine. He showed everybody a tube of rock tailing that had flecks of real gold in it. And he talked about the fight he'd got into in the bar in Hay River on his way back home.

"Those white boys were calling me out," he said. "Hank backed me up, and we whipped their ass but good." To Bud Peyen, it was a shared victory.

My father returned home with confirmation that he was completely unsuited for what he called "the rewarding and challenging field of manual labour." This was meant as a joke, but my mother didn't think it was very funny. Things were starting to feel tense around our house, and it didn't help matters when my father spent the last of my parents' money on a failed partnership in a snack bar in High Level. All he got out of that was the left-over unsold stock. Although his children were thrilled when he showed up with cases of grape pop and boxes of chips, his wife wasn't happy.

"Henry," my mother said, "we can't go on like this. You need to find a job, a real job. We need money."

When the wolf comes calling at the door, love flies out the window. Or at least that's what my father always said. He'd mumble it under his breath whenever my mother brought up the family finances. But he decided he had no choice. He had to go back to teaching. He wouldn't be able to work for Gene Rogers any more, but the public school was hiring. Once he had the proper accreditation, he'd be able to get, as my mother had put it, a real job.

My father was accepted into the University of Saskatchewan in Regina. He was going to earn his degree, become a legal teacher, then come back, as he told my mother one night when he thought we were asleep, and "shove that diploma right up Gene Rogers's ass."

The decision was announced to us the next morning at break-fast. We played dumb, although we already knew what was going to happen. We'd taken to listening at the top of the stairs, since we weren't used to hearing our parents fight. It was making us all feel nervous. My brother Dan, in particular, was finding it hard to sleep at night. It was a relief to hear the news. We were going south.

The night before we left there was a Tea Dance in town. We could hear the drums, but we weren't allowed to go; we were too busy packing. We loaded up the car the next morning. My father wanted to board up the windows and put a padlock on our front door, but my mother told him not to bother. She didn't think anybody would come into our house while we were away, and he ended up agreeing. Or maybe just didn't feel like doing the work. It's not as if we had much to steal.

You might think a long drive in a car full of kids would be unpleasant. It wasn't. Everybody was excited, and every time we passed through a new town, my brother Sean would announce, "Well, we've never been *this* far south before." We sang songs and took turns telling stories, and we were having a wonderful time. Then the Zephyr started making a clunking sound.

My mother and father paused mid-smile. "What's that noise?" my mother asked.

"It's nothing," my father said.

"The car's never made that noise before," my mother said.

The clunking got louder. Then it stopped.

"See," my father said, "it's nothing."

"I think you should pull over and take a look," said my mother.

My father rolled his eyes. I could see him in the rearview mirror. He obviously thought there was nothing to worry about. But he pulled the car over to the side of the road, turned it off, got out, and opened the hood. The rest of us gathered around as he stood pretending to look at the engine.

"What's wrong with it?" My mother was holding up my brother Billy, who wanted to see the motor.

"Seems fine," my father said. "Who needs to go to the bathroom?"

We all did, so off into the bushes we went. We got back into the Zephyr, and my father put the key in the ignition. The motor didn't turn over. It did make a coughing noise, more like a death rattle, and then it was silent.

"Wonderful," my father said, and then, to my mother, "you're the one who wanted me to stop." Like it was her fault.

"You're the one who drove the car up into the Territories," she said. Like it was his fault.

We had to push the car before it would start. My father shoved on the open driver's door, my mother stretched her leg over and put her foot on the clutch, and Dan, Sean and I threw our combined weight against the rear bumper. Even Billy helped out; he sat in my mother's lap yelling, "Faster, faster!" The motor finally caught, and the moment it sputtered to life, my father climbed into the car to keep it running. It kept moving, too, and Dan, Sean and I had to chase after it, pull open the rear doors, and scramble inside. The instant we closed our doors, my father stepped on the gas.

We drove in silence, until we'd got our wind back, and then my father spoke up.

"The next time we have to do that," he said, "let's make sure we leave the back doors open."

My mother looked over at my father.

"It'll be easier for the boys to climb back inside," my father said.

We didn't have to push the car every single time we stopped. Unless we were getting gas, my father would leave the motor running. My mother would race into a store to buy food, and everybody would charge into the washroom and out again as quickly as we could. We became very efficient at pushing the car when we had to, although Billy's contribution became less and less appreciated. He'd shout out "Faster." And the rest of us, including my father, would shout "Shut up!"

Eventually, though, the Zephyr gave up the ghost. We'd driven all the previous day and through most of the night. The sun was starting to come up again. Everybody was asleep except for my dad and me.

"Welcome to Saskatchewan," my father said.

"Mmph," I said. I was awake, but still sleepy.

"We just crossed the border," my father said.

"Clunk." That was the Zephyr. The sound wasn't that loud. It was the silence that followed that woke everyone else up.

We spent the morning in Lloydminster, while my father tried to figure out a way to get us back on the road. He couldn't afford repairs, so he went off to find someone to con. It didn't take him that long. We'd only been waiting in the car with my mother for a few hours when he showed up riding in the cab of a bright yellow tow truck. A moon-faced man was driving. Fred Koch, the man's name turned out to be. Fred backed his truck into position, hopped out, and hooked up the Zephyr. He seemed a happy sort, and he had the twinkliest blue eyes. My mother was about to say something to him when my father caught her eye and gave a small shake of his head.

Fred Koch operated a garage in Lloydminster. I don't know what kind of line my father had fed him, but it must have been a good one, because he didn't tow us to his shop; he took us to his farm on the outskirts of town. His wife, Lena, was waiting for us, and she seemed even friendlier than Fred was. She brought all of us into her kitchen for soup and sandwiches and fresh milk right from the cow. Then she took us out to the barn to look at the animals. The Kochs had a purebred beagle with a new litter of puppies, so that occupied our attention.

By the time my father came out to the barn to collect us, he had moved our bags and belongings into a midnight blue Volkswagen station wagon. The station wagon was parked next to our car, facing the direction of the highway, and it was about half the size of the Zephyr, inside and out. We squeezed into the car, barely, and my father made sure we all said a proper thank-you to Mr. and Mrs. Koch for their hospitality. As we were about to leave, Mrs. Koch presented my mother with one of the beagle puppies.

"For the children, yes?" she said.

"Oh, we couldn't," said my mother.

My father slapped on his largest smile. "Of course we can," he said.

My brothers and I cheered. As we drove away, still waving, the smile dropped from my father's face.

"Great," he said. "Another mouth to feed."

My father had said something to Fred Koch about making sure he had his address and getting in touch soon. If the Volkswagen was a loaner, though, we never gave it back.

The trip became fun again, even in the cramped circumstances. All the dogs we knew in Fort Vermilion were working animals. We didn't think of them as pets. But here we'd been given our very own puppy. My dad had got us a new car and our first-ever pet, and he'd done it in half a day. I was proud of him. My mother didn't seem happy, but I figured that was because the puppy kept peeing on the car seat.

We deked around Saskatoon and kept going south, all the way to the Standing Buffalo Reserve. My father had got a job teaching adult-education classes there on the weekends, and free housing was part of the deal. We moved into a prefabricated house on the road leading into the reserve, across a field from the school. My father commuted to Regina to attend university. He had a full course load, and he also graded papers for any professor who would hire him. Actually, my mother did the grading.

Standing Buffalo was nothing but rolling hills and prairie grass. Not a tree in sight, whichever way you looked. Small houses were tucked up in the hills and hidden in the valleys. It was so different from Fort Vermilion. Even the Indians weren't like the ones we'd grown up with. These Indians were Sioux, descendants of the survivors of the great victory of Little Big Horn who had chosen Canada as a new home. They didn't look Beaver or Cree. They looked like the Indians in movies. They didn't have the brushcuts we were used to seeing; they wore their hair long and braided. The people were poor, that part was the same, but they were also friendly. We'd barely moved in when the first kid arrived, asking me if I wanted to come out and play. By the time the summer ended, Clyde Yuzichipi was my new best friend. School began, and I fell head over heels for Mrs. Greyeyes, the first Indian schoolteacher I'd ever met.

One really bad thing did happen. Our beagle had turned out to be a timid little dog that would pee on the floor if you looked at it sideways. I can't recall the name we gave it, which is probably for the best, since the school bus driver ran over our dog when it wandered out onto the road. Second day of school, too. So that was the end of our first dog, but it was also how we got our new one. The bus driver felt so terrible he turned his school bus around and headed to the opposite side of the reserve. He brought us back a puppy, a black fuzzball of cuteness we called Wakan Tonka, which we thought was the Sioux word for "large" or "big." Mrs. Greyeyes told me it actually meant "the Creator," and she suggested we rename the dog Ta Tonka, "Big Buffalo," which we eventually shortened to Tonka. The name was meant to be ironic, but the dog fooled us. Tonka was half German shepherd and half coyote, although it took us a while to figure that out, and he topped the scales at over sixty pounds when he finally finished growing.

The new sister we got a couple of weeks later was more or less completely grown already. My father had been married before he met my mother, and he had an ex-wife and a teenaged daughter living in Regina. Margaret, our new sister, wasn't a surprise to us; my mother had met Margaret when she was a little girl, and we'd seen pictures of her. But we were a complete surprise to Margaret. Apparently, our father had never got around to passing along our pictures to her.

We were crazy about Margaret from the start. She came for a visit first, and then she moved in with us on Standing Buffalo. She became good friends with my mother, who in turn became quite friendly with Margaret's mom. Margaret and her mom had been fighting all the time, teenager stuff, and my mother suggested Margaret spend some time with us. My father didn't like the idea, but Margaret's mother and my mother outvoted him. So now we had a new big sister, and she was terrific. For one thing, she let us read her comic books.

Our other new sister came home from the hospital with my mother, which seemed to be how those things worked. We fell madly in love with Lorna Joan, who was round and wrinkled and who giggled and gurgled and who was given the unfortunate nickname of "Pruney" by our father. He said she looked exactly like a prune when she arrived, and the name would follow her into adulthood. My parents brought Lorna Joan home from the hospital, but my mother hadn't actually given birth to her. Lorna Joan's birth mother lived on the reserve, she was pregnant, she didn't believe she could raise the baby, she and my mother were friends, and that was that. Now there were six of us kids. My mother has this great photo of my big sister Margaret holding my baby sister Lorna Joan after a day of exhausting babysitting. My big sister looks as if a truck ran over her and then backed up to try again. My baby sister looks as if she was the one driving the truck.

The Christmas we spent on Standing Buffalo was our best one ever. Not because there were lots of presents under the tree—that didn't happen—but because we were having such a splendid time. Two new sisters, a new dog, even, for me, a new best friend. I saw my first play on Standing Buffalo, Globe Theatre's *The*

Mirror Man. It was a great children's show in which two actors played the same character, or rather one played the character and one played his reflection. I got to be part of the play when one of the actors tripped over me and fell down. We thought it was part of the show.

My mother helped the women on the reserve organize the Tah-hah-shee-nah Rug Co-op, which made hooked rugs using traditional Sioux designs. The co-op was a way for the very poor reserve to bring in money, and it returned some of the power back to the women, where it belonged. The members of the rug co-op sold their art all over the world, and they and my mother were invited to New York City to show their rugs at the New York Trade Fair. Their success got them some attention in Canada, and a National Film Board crew was sent out to the reserve to make a documentary. The documentary is called *Standing Buffalo,* and it is still available from the NFB. If you watch it you'll see me run naked across a room. You can see my brother Billy without his clothes on, too.

We would have enjoyed our life in Saskatchewan if we had stayed on the Standing Buffalo Reserve. But we were only there for one summer and half a winter. My father got tired of travelling back and forth, so he quit his weekend job teaching adult education and picked up some work teaching night classes on campus. We moved to Regina on New Year's Day, 1969. Suddenly we were living in the big city. Everything seemed to speed up.

My parents got caught up in the spirit of the times. My mother found a job managing the first daycare centre at the university, and she became friends with a pair of fanatical Marxist-Leninists with the last name of Gortny. They had a son they'd named Gorky. Gorky Gortny. How would you like to go through life with that handle? I'm willing to bet he long ago changed his name to something sensible, like George.

My father, in addition to working on his degree and teaching night classes, wrote articles for Regina's alternative newspaper, the *Prairie Fire*. They hired my brother Dan as their editorial cartoonist, and it is a widely accepted family legend that Dan was investigated by the RCMP, who were a tad surprised to discover he was only thirteen years old.

It was the height of the Vietnam War, and I was once on the front page of the *Leader-Post* marching in a demonstration with my mother to protest a performance by the United States Marine Corps Band. In the photo, I'm holding one half of a banner that reads "Crime in Cambodia, Culture in Canada, Boycott the U.S. Army Band." Not one hundred per cent accurate, but fervently felt. My family ended up as part of an underground railroad, meaning we would open our doors to draft dodgers and deserters. One fellow taught my brother Dan how to throw a proper side kick, and Dan broke a closet door clean in half.

We lived in the north end of Regina at 1211 Retalleck Street. It wasn't a good address then, and it hasn't changed. The house reeked of our poverty. We may not have had much money in Fort Vermilion, but we never missed a meal. There were times on Retalleck Street when we went to bed hungry. My mother's salary from the daycare and the money from my father's night classes didn't stretch far enough, especially now that we didn't have free housing. Agitating and protesting didn't pay a thing. I was getting into fights and being chased home after school, only it wasn't Ted Carrier throwing the punches. This time it was white kids doing the chasing. My brothers and I stood out. We wore shabby clothes and we talked funny. We were fair game.

My father started coming home later and later. He was barely around. I don't remember my parents fighting during this time; they simply stopped talking to each other. My sister Margaret had lots to say to my father, however, and she didn't say it quietly.

The two of them only had to be in the same room for a few seconds before an argument would break out.

One time my father simply didn't come home. He was gone all day Saturday and all day Sunday. We were in bed asleep when the front door slammed on Monday night. It made the walls shudder. My father was trying to be quiet, but we could hear him as he came stumbling up the stairs. He went room to room to give us all a kiss goodnight. I pretended to be asleep, but I could smell the alcohol on him. He went in to join my mother, and they had a long, hissing argument that lasted well into the morning. My father had started drinking again. He never stopped after that. He eventually died from it. Cirrhosis.

The argument continued for the next few days. My mother had decided she didn't like Regina, didn't like the people my father was hanging out with. She wanted to go home. My father thought this was ridiculous. What did she want him to do with his life? Be a schoolteacher, for God's sake? He was meeting people, smart people, important people. That's why he stayed out so late. Didn't she see that everything he did was for the future? There were opportunities for a sharp fellow like him here in the city. What he needed was some support, and if my mother would stop being so negative all the time, if she'd stop being such a wet blanket, things would work out fine.

"So much love, so little understanding," said my father. He tossed that at my mother, and it shut her up. It didn't shut up my big sister Margaret, though. She laced into my father so fiercely he told her to get out and go back to her real mother. That shut my sister up but good. The rest of us just tried to get out of the way. We weren't happy when Margaret packed up her things, and she was crying when she kissed us good-bye.

About five years ago, I got around to asking my mother what had really happened in Regina. She took a while to think about it, then responded in a thoughtful manner.

"Your father got tired of the long con. Those first ten years we had together were the best ten years of my life, but he was only pretending to be that person, to be a good husband and a good father and a good teacher, and after a while he couldn't pretend any more. When we moved to Regina, he decided it was time to pretend to be someone else."

We left Saskatchewan before the end of our second summer there. My mother packed us up and took us away. We kids were sent to the movies, which was a rare occurrence, and by the time we got back, the Volkswagen was loaded and ready to go. My father showed up at the last possible second, and my mother got out of the car to say something to him. He reached for her, but she pulled her hand away and got back into the car. My mother and five children and a large dog stuffed into the smallest station wagon ever manufactured. My brothers and my sister and I turned around to wave farewell to our father. He stood there getting smaller and smaller as we drove away. I could feel my eyes burning, so I twisted back around. My brother Dan was sitting in front of me in the passenger's seat, staring straight ahead. We were off. We were travelling. We were heading home.

TEA DANCE

Going home felt twice as long as the trip out had. We had left Regina in the evening, and we drove through the night before finally pulling into a campground outside of Edmonton, where my mother took a nap and the rest of us tried to wake up. We took Tonka for a walk around the campground, since we were the only people there, and then we tied him up to a picnic table and I tried to get my brother Dan to tell me what was going on.

"How come we're going back to the Fort?"

"Because we have a house there."

"We had a house in Regina."

"The house in Fort Vermilion doesn't cost us anything."

"Well, okay, how come Dad isn't coming with us?"

"You'll figure it out when you're older," my brother said. "Now stop being such a baby."

He turned around and went back to the car. It was the worst thing he could have said. He should have punched me. A baby? I wasn't acting like a baby; I was trying to figure out what was happening. And when I say he should have punched me instead, I don't want to leave you with the impression that Dan and I didn't fight. Later that year, he would hit me in the mouth and break one of my teeth, and I would retaliate by throwing a rock at his head and sending him to the hospital for six stitches. He still has that scar, and I still have that chipped tooth.

I decided to do something I was good at, which was to go away and sulk. I wanted to get as far away from my family as possible, maybe even out of sight. That would show them. My mother would want to know where I had gone, and my brother Dan would have to tell her he had been mean to me, and wouldn't he be sorry then?

The problem was, before I could get far enough away, my brother Sean brought my brother Billy down to see me. My mother had finished her nap by now and was splashing water on her face from an outdoor tap. My brothers found that boring, since it meant we were probably going to have to get back in the car again, and that meant more driving, which was the most boring thing of all. My mother would have to change Lorna Joan's diaper first, and that was no fun to watch. Also, my brother Sean wanted to know if I knew what was going on with my parents and why everybody was in such a bad mood.

"You'll understand when you're older," I said. "Now, go back up to the car."

Sean and Billy had started to walk away when my mother started yelling.

"Get in the car," she said, and she was really screaming at me. "Get the boys and get in the car."

I started to run towards her.

"No, don't run, just walk."

I stopped moving.

"Quickly! Walk quickly!"

Sean and Billy had almost made it to the car. I would have continued in that direction myself, but Tonka was making a huge
racket, and I wanted to see why. He was pulling at his chain so
hard his front legs were off the ground, and he was growling in
a way he'd never done before. My entire family had started
screaming and shouting, but all that made me do was run around
in circles, towards the dog and back again. Then I saw the bear.

It wasn't a grizzly, and I doubt it was even a full-grown black
bear, but it was plenty big enough, and it was heading right for
me. It wasn't walking on all fours, either. It was up on its hind
legs. If you had any knowledge of bear lore, which we did from
growing up in the North, you knew that was a bad sign. It was an
even worse sign when my family stopped making noise. It was as
if someone had thrown a switch, and then I heard my mother,
who was trying to speak in a calm and reassuring manner.

"Whatever you do," she said, "don't run. Don't move fast.
Just start backing away from the bear."

Easier said than done. I was terrified, and I was worried I was
going to pee my pants. I took a careful step backwards. The bear
took one big step forward. I took one more step backwards, and I
tripped over a root and fell down. The bear took this as a sign of
weakness and charged. Everybody screamed at the same time,
and I closed my eyes, because, really, did I want to watch myself
being eaten? No, thank you.

When I opened my eyes a second later, the bear was gone. So
was the dog. Tonka had snapped his chain and, instead of doing
the sensible thing and running to the car, he had charged. He'd
attacked the bear with such ferocity that the bear had wheeled
around and gone crashing into the woods. Followed by Tonka.

My mother ran down and grabbed me and pulled me to my
feet. She dragged me to the car, paying no attention to what I was

saying, which was mainly things like "Ouch," and "That hurts," and "Let go of me." She got us all into the relative safety of the Volkswagen, and then she started the engine. This didn't go over too well.

"Noooooo," we said.

"We can't go," we said.

"We have to wait for Tonka to come back," we said.

"I hate you," I said, but I didn't mean it. It was just that our dog had saved my life, and it seemed like a rotten trick to drive off and leave him there. My mother was under enough stress already, what with leaving her husband and driving all night and worrying about the future and everything, but she capitulated. We sat in the car, with the motor running in case the bear came back and we had to make a quick getaway, and we waited for Tonka to return.

Which he did, about half an hour later, looking very pleased with himself and none the worse for wear. He was a hero, and he got a hero's reception from us, with much hugging and patting and many compliments on his bravery. No one mentioned my lack of grace under pressure, and that was good, since I was hoping nobody would notice that I had, just a little, and it's perfectly understandable given the circumstances, peed my pants.

When I later told the story to Lloyd Loonskin, I left out that part. I made the bear a whole lot bigger. And I made myself a whole lot braver. Tonka was still the hero, however.

"Yeah, you got yourself a good dog there, partner."

"He's the best dog in the world."

"I dunno," said Lloyd Loonskin, "can he pull a sled?"

"I bet he could if he wanted to," I said. "He'd have to be a lead dog, though."

Sled dogs are big and strong and dumb. A sled dog will keep running until his heart explodes. Lead dogs are smaller and smarter and faster. They don't actually pull anything. They guide the team. A good lead dog will run only until he gets tired, then he takes a break. I figured that was the sort of job my dog would be good at.

I had been regaling Lloyd Loonskin and anybody else who would listen with stories about my adventures in the big city. The city may have been Regina, but it was bigger than Peace River, and most of the kids in town hadn't even been there. Some of the white kids had been to places like Toronto and Calgary, and we hadn't gone to Edmonton, we'd only driven through, but I didn't care. I wasn't trying to impress the white kids.

"There was a store that sold nothing but comic books, and we got to go to a movie theatre, a real movie theatre, and you could ride a bus and go all over the city, anywhere you wanted, and there was a place right around the corner from our house where you could take empty pop bottles and they would give you money and the guy who ran it was, I think, Chinese or something. Anyway, he was a real nice guy."

"Yeah."

Lloyd Loonskin didn't seem to be enjoying my stories that day. He'd heard them a few times before, but that didn't seem like a good reason for being so grumpy.

"Man, you're owly," I said. "What's wrong with you?"

"There's nothing wrong with *me*," he said.

"What are you talking about, you dummy?"

"Yeah, well, you've been long gone, you," Lloyd Loonskin said, "two summers and one winter since we seen you, and, well . . ."

"What?"

"Since you come back from the city, you're acting pretty cheeky, you."

Now, this was one of the worst things you could say about anyone. Acting cheeky meant you were full of yourself, cocky, arrogant.

"You're just mad about Clyde Yuzichipi," I said.

"Who?"

"Yeah, right," I said. It was obvious Lloyd Loonskin was jealous.

"All you ever do is talk about yourself," said Lloyd Loonskin.

"I'm telling you what happened to me."

"Yeah, well, stuff happened to me, too, okay?"

I was tempted to be sharp in my reply, something along the lines of "Oh, yeah?" or "Sure it did," but I was just sensitive enough to shut up.

"Yeah. We got to move, my grandmother and me," said Lloyd Loonskin.

While we'd been gone from Fort Vermilion, something major had occurred. The Catholic Church had sold their land to two businessmen, and the two businessmen had evicted everybody who lived on that land. Those people were squatters, it seemed, even though some of their houses had been built almost a century earlier. Nobody had ever thought to buy land or bother with who owned it. People would build a small house, usually out of squared-off logs, then chink it up with mud, maybe whitewash it, and move in. This had been going on for many generations, until the Catholic Church decided to sell the land to speculators.

One of these speculators was a Metis, Frank Jones. Frank Jones had money. Real money. He was what you might call a Professional Indian, well known and well liked by the politicians down in Edmonton. He wore suits and ties and he combed his hair straight back from his forehead. He was average-sized, but he looked smaller than he was. His shoulders might have had something to do with that; he didn't appear to have any. Bankers, lawyers, white people in general got along with Frank Jones fine. He could sit down in a fancy restaurant and use the right fork. The Indians didn't think much of him. Bud Peyen called him an "Uncle Tomahawk."

"His name should be Frank McIntosh," Bud Peyen said. "He's red on the outside and white on the inside, like the apple."

Frank Jones was able to turn a good profit in Fort Vermilion. He had an exclusive contract for road repair in the area, and he had convinced the provincial government to pay for his graders and gravel trucks. He owned the only gas pumps in town, and now he was bound and determined to open a hotel. Not that Fort Vermilion needed one—we didn't get that many visitors—but Frank Jones knew that building a hotel would give him the right to open a licensed beverage room. That would be a beer parlour, also known as a tavern or a bar.

Frank Jones was going to bring alcohol to Fort Vermilion. He was doing a service to the community. No longer would thirsty people have to travel all the way to High Level to have a drink at the Northgate Hotel; they could stay right in town. Be a lot less drunk driving that way. Also, he was going to call the hotel the Sheridan Lawrence Motor Hotel, after one of the early pioneers to settle in the area, so that added a historical dimension to the operation. The only land he deemed suitable, being right downtown, was the land the Catholic Church owned. Was he concerned about the thirty or so families that were going to be evicted? Nope. The government was building them brand-new houses.

The Alberta Housing Corporation, backed by the Central Mortgage and Housing Corporation, was going to build the houses. CMHC was building homes for Indians right across the country. The houses were hastily designed, cheaply made and hurriedly built. They represented an attempt by the government of Canada to get the aboriginal population out of the bush and into buildings that looked more like the government's idea of real residences. This was also seen as a good way to add the logic and order of street addresses, something that had heretofore been missing. The houses came with oil heaters, electricity and outdoor toilets. They built twenty-four of them in Fort Vermilion, all identical in design, but each with a different paint job, to encourage individuality and pride of neighbourhood. The development looked, Bud Peyen said, "like the kind of place where even if a fellow comes home sober he won't be able to find his own home."

Nobody wanted to move into the new houses, despite the added amenities. Bud Peyen decided to disassemble his cabin and move it deeper into the woods. But most people didn't have that kind of initiative or ability. Lloyd Loonskin was worried about his grandmother. She'd lived in her house for over sixty years. She'd been born there. So had Lloyd Loonskin.

"Where we live now, my grandma can walk to the post office or to the store. If we move to this new place, it's gonna be too far for her to walk."

The new housing development was way out on the edge of town, a good three or four miles from anything. The land it was built on was owned by Warren Pritchard, a recent arrival in Fort Vermilion. Warren Pritchard and Frank Jones were partners. Frank bought land from the Church to build his hotel. Warren sold land to the government so they could build houses. The timing was suspiciously perfect. The evictions were announced one month before the Central Mortgage and Housing Corporation made their big announcement. Warren Pritchard and Frank Jones may or may not have been shrewd businessmen, but they had friends where it counted.

"I don't get it," said Lloyd Loonskin. "Why does everything have to change?"

My mother always said later that that's when the town went downhill. After the evictions, it was never the same place again. Father Litzler took a lot of heat, but he had nothing to do with the Church's decision. He was as upset about it as anybody else. Bud Peyen turned to Augustus Noskiye for spiritual guidance.

"Remember," said the old Medicine Man, "some white people are good, and some white people are not so good."

"Frank Jones is building the hotel. He's going to sell booze."

"Well, some Indians are not so good as well," said Augustus Noskiye. "I'll pray for Frank Jones."

"Pray his liquor licence doesn't come through," said Bud Peyen.

Frank Jones stopped by our house the odd time, but he never made it past the front door. My mother was now a single parent with five kids. She owned land. This made her the most eligible woman in town, and there was plenty of interest being shown. Bud Peyen put a stop to the unwanted visitors by regularly dropping off moose meat for my mother. Some folks got the impression my mother and Bud were interested in each other. Most people didn't believe it, but nobody wanted to take a chance and step on Bud's moccasins. Even Frank Jones called it quits. There wasn't anything romantic going on, though. Bud had simply noticed she didn't have any meat hanging in her trees. Since most homes had no electricity, and that meant no refrigeration, meat was smoked in the summer to preserve it, then left outdoors to freeze solid in the winter. Meat that was smoked was covered in wax paper to help draw out the moisture and keep flies away, and meat that got frozen was wrapped up in cheesecloth. Either way, it ended up in a tree to protect it from scavengers. You could tell how well a family was doing by walking past their yard and seeing how much meat was up in their trees.

After we returned from Saskatchewan without my father in tow, Bud Peyen had become alarmed at the total lack of tree meat on our property and had taken to bringing over game whenever he could. My mother could have pointed out that we now had electricity, and that one of the last purchases she and my father had made together was an electric fridge from the Eaton's catalogue—

a move that annoyed Scott Wagner at the Hudson's Bay no end—but she didn't. We were broke, and our food was coming from our vegetable garden and Bud Peyen's generosity. The only cost of his deliveries was that he would ask the same question of my mother every time.

"Louise, have you heard from Hank at all?"

"No, Bud, not one word."

"Not a letter or nothing?"

"No, Bud, I'm sorry, but nothing."

"Well, maybe soon he'll write, him."

"You never know."

"Or maybe he's gonna phone, him."

My mother didn't have a telephone, but Ellen McAteer did, and she lived close enough to come and get my mother if there was a call. That's what Bud Peyen figured.

"Oh, I don't think he'll call, Bud."

"But maybe."

"Stranger things have happened."

"Well, if he calls, you know, maybe you tell him I said hello."

"I'll do that Bud, if he calls," said my mother. "And thank you for the moose meat."

Nobody in town blinked at my brand-new baby sister. Lorna Joan was obviously some kind of Indian, but most people figured she was the result of a fling. Even Bud Peyen thought my mother had maybe switched blankets while we were out of town, but she set him right.

"Well, Louise, people think she's your kid, you know."

"Bud," said my mother, "Lorna Joan *is* my daughter." She tried to explain the principles involved in an open adoption, but Bud Peyen found them too difficult to follow. He shrugged it off.

"You want me to straighten everybody out?"

"No, you can leave it be. Anybody who believes it isn't someone who knows me very well."

"Don't take offence at it, anyways," said Bud Peyen.

"I won't, Bud," said my mother. "And thanks for the venison."

My mother got herself hired part-time at the hospital to do bookkeeping and paperwork. It didn't pay a lot, but we made do. If you didn't have meat for a stew, you could always burn flour and salt and add it to the broth. It tasted exactly like beef. Thanks to Bud Peyen's meat deliveries, we didn't have to eat burnt-flour stew too often.

Lloyd Loonskin and I celebrated our eleventh birthdays together. We had to go down to his new house, because his grandmother couldn't make the walk up the hill. She was getting very old, and Lloyd was missing lots of school to stay with her. Neither of us got much in the way of presents. Lloyd's grandmother gave him a shirt she'd sewed, but it didn't fit him right. My mother took me to one side and gave me a letter she'd written. It was a secret, she said, and I had to promise not to show it to anyone else, and never to tell my brothers or my sister what it said. The letter talked about how much she loved me and told me I was her favourite. Each of us ended up getting the same letter, but we didn't figure that out until years later. It wasn't a bad birthday. There was a cake, with candles for Lloyd and me to blow out.

"Make a wish," my mother said.

I don't know what Lloyd Loonskin wished for, although he'd have told me if I'd asked. Maybe he wished for a bicycle, or a hockey stick, or maybe for his grandmother to feel better. I wished that my father hadn't missed my birthday. He missed all of the birthdays that year.

Christmas was tough, too. Nobody got any presents, and you could tell my mom felt bad about that. We tried to make her feel better by pretending that we were too old for toys and stuff. We even went so far as to tell her we didn't believe in Santa Claus any more, but we made sure not to say that if Lorna Joan or Billy was around. We were trying to cheer her up. I'm not sure it worked.

We made it through the holidays, and then it was back to school. Winter went by, then a summer, then another winter, then one more summer. We didn't get a single letter from my father, let alone a phone call.

My brother Dan tried to step in as the man of the household, but he wasn't good at it. He wasn't old enough to get a job, and his idea of helping my mother was to yell at us for not helping out more. She was working full-time at the hospital now, which meant more money but longer hours. She'd finish work, then come home and get us fed and cleaned up and ready for the next day. One time, she came through the front door so tired she could barely make it to a chair. Dan had a cup of tea waiting. He brought it over to her, and she smiled.

"Well," said my mother, "it's good to be home."

"Oh," said my big brother, "is that what this is?"

My mother's eyes went angry. It looked for a second as if she might throw her tea at him.

"Yes," she said. "That's what this is. Our home. We live here."

She bit the words out, and you could tell from her voice that she was mad. Dan got a hurt look on his face. I didn't feel sorry for him. As far as I was concerned, he was asking for it. What reason did he have to be so crabby?

I was about to say something mean to my brother when the front door was flung open and Ellen McAteer came marching in. She wasn't being rude. Most people didn't lock their doors. Most front doors didn't have locks, in fact, and although it was considered good manners to knock before entering, Ellen was in a big hurry because she had big news.

"Louise," she said, "you better get over to my house this second."

"What is it, Ellen?"

"You've got a phone call. It's Hank. Your husband is on the line."

My mother made good time following Ellen McAteer out the door. It seemed as if she was gone for a week. When she returned, it was hard to tell anything from her face. She still looked mostly tired.

"Your father is coming home," she said.

None of us could think what to say. I looked over at Dan. He was happy, I suppose, although it was hard to tell with him.

"When's he coming?" I asked.

"Soon," my mother said.

"How long is that?"

"As soon as he gets here," said my mother.

Three days later, I arrived home from school in a bit of a hurry. Ted Carrier was chasing me. I made it safely into our yard, although I almost ran right into a strange car. A big Chevrolet Biscayne was parked in front of our house. I could put a name to every vehicle in town, but I hadn't seen this one before. I had an idea who that car belonged to, and I couldn't wait to see if I was right.

"This is your new sister," my father said. "Her name is Darla Jean."

My father was sitting in one of the kitchen chairs. My brother Billy was clasping him tight around the neck, and my sister Lorna Joan sat on his lap. My mother was holding a small Indian girl. I didn't get a good look at her because I was too busy whooping and hollering and jumping up and down. My brother Sean joined me; he was some glad to see our dad as well. Once we'd got that out of our systems, we introduced ourselves to Darla Jean, and all the kissing and hugging about scared her to death.

"Where'd she come from?" I asked my father.

"I found her under a sugar beet," he said.

My father had gone into a new line of work, it seemed. He was managing a United Church project called Operation Mustard Seed, after the Biblical reference, a sort of clearing house for the socially disadvantaged, offering literacy classes, alcohol and drug counselling, job preparation training and the latest in catch phrases and trends: life skills education. My father figured he'd make a killing, and if he did some good at the same time, that wouldn't hurt anybody. In one of his impassioned pitch sessions, he had referred with such vehemence to the Third World conditions most of Canada's Indian population lived in that he was hired to escort a television crew to the sugar beet fields of southern Alberta.

It was bad. The camera crew were both disturbed and elated. Disturbed because none of them had ever seen human beings living in that kind of squalor, and elated because the pictures of that shantytown were going to make for good television. My father was their designated dog robber, meaning he functioned as a combination guide and go-between. He had already seen conditions as bad as the ones in the sugar beet fields.

That's where he found my sister Darla, he said. He'd been bragging to everybody he met about how smart his sons and daughter were and what a good mother his wife was. We sounded like such a great family that people started begging him to take their children away and raise them in a proper home. That's what he told us, anyway.

"I had a dozen children to choose from," my father said. "But I knew your mother wanted another girl, so I eliminated all the boys."

I looked over at my mother. She didn't seem to be enjoying the story, but she did seem to be enjoying her new daughter.

"So there were six little girls, and I made sure I picked the best one." My father finished his story and winked at me. He knew I was old enough to understand. "She was hiding underneath a sugar beet, and I dug her out of the ground and brought her home."

That last part might have been true. Darla Jean did look as if she needed a good scrubbing. Wherever she came from, they must not have fed her much, because she would sneak bread crusts off the table and hide them under her mattress. It took her a long time to quit that habit.

My brother Dan came home late from school, so he missed the best part of the celebration. My father seemed really glad to see him.

"Come here," he said. "Give your father a kiss."

My brother didn't move from the doorway.

"Come on, son," my father said. "Come over here."

"Henry," my mother said, "leave him be."

My father had to settle for a brisk manly handshake with my big brother. That night our newest sister slept with my mother in her room downstairs. So did my father. We could hear a whispered conversation going on between them. My brother Dan and I tiptoed down the stairs for a better listen, but we couldn't make out the words, so we gave up and went back to bed.

"This is the best day ever," I said.

"Right," my brother said.

"We got a new sister," I said, "and Dad's back."

Dan punched me in the arm and rolled over to go to sleep. He didn't hit me very hard, though. He must have been tired from the excitement.

The next day, Dad left us again. He explained that he had come by only to drop off our new sister. He had his job to get back to in the city. He shook hands with Dan, gave my mother a kiss on the cheek, and hugged the rest of us. He pulled out of the yard, gave the horn a couple of jaunty toots, and drove off. My brother Dan stood in the yard listening to the sound of the car fading away. He stayed out there long after the rest of us had gone back inside to warm up. He wasn't crying; he didn't even look that sad. He was simply waiting, as if he thought something was going to happen, as if the sound of the car might suddenly get louder and louder and my father would have changed his mind and turned around and come back like the whole thing was a joke. Or maybe Dan knew something the rest of us didn't. My father never came back to Fort Vermilion. We didn't hear from him for another year, and some of his children wouldn't see him again for a decade.

We heard the drums calling out that night, and we followed the sound to Sylvester Paul's house. We hadn't been to a Tea Dance since we left for the South. There hadn't been so many of them in the past few years, and I'd almost forgotten how much fun it was to go. There were the drummers and there were the singers and there was everybody else, old people and young people, in the circle doing that shuffling broken-legged step. The circle kept going and going and you could dance all night and never get tired, never need to sit down. It smelled of wood smoke and moccasin leather and tobacco. It was the same as it had ever been, and it felt like home.

Sylvester Paul had been one of my father's students, and one of the first members of his Boy Scout troop. He was happy to hear my dad had come for a visit, and sad that he had left again so soon. Bud Peyen was even sadder, because my dad hadn't gone to see him.

"Bud asks about you all the time," I had said to my father the night he was home.

"Who's that?" It was a few seconds before a look of recognition passed over his face. "Oh, Bud," he said. "My old sidekick. I haven't thought about him in ages."

I didn't understand how you could forget about someone as big as Bud Peyen.

nine

THROAT SINGER

I*t was the prettiest song* you'd ever want to hear. The first time it was played was at the Fort Vermilion Talent Show, which was the climactic event of the annual Winter Carnival. The Winter Carnival consisted of sled dog races on the Peace River, bannock-making competitions, and the flour-packing contest, which Bud Peyen had won so many times he was barred from official competition. The Winter Carnival was the highlight of the Fort Vermilion social calendar, and it was one of the few times that everyone in town would get together. The entire population would pack into the Legion Hall for the talent show, hooting and hollering, cheering the good performances and catcalling the less talented acts. One year a skinny teenager from a farm across the river was led out onstage. He announced he was going to sing a tune that he himself had made up. He started playing his guitar and singing, and we all knew that was the best damn song we'd ever heard.

Country girl, yes she was
Like wildflowers, on the plain
She needs the country
Like the country
Needs the rain

David Boire was blind. It started with an accident, when he got stuck in the right eye with a shard of metal that popped off a combine harvester. The eye became infected, and the blindness spread to his left eye, and there he was, nine or ten years old, and what was he going to do with himself? What he did was go on to be a great big star. Don't feel bad that you've never heard of him.

David Boire taught himself how to play the guitar. You could say my mother had something to do with his songwriting career, since she took enough of an interest to get some books brought in so he could learn Braille. David Boire did so well with his guitar-playing and songwriting and singing that he ended up with his own band, David Boire and the Mustangs. They were a big draw all over northern Alberta—from Peace River to Manning to Grimshaw—and all the way up to Yellowknife. The Mustangs were a cover band; they did their own versions of well-known country songs, and the drummer would let loose once a show with a spirited rendition of "Wipe Out." Whenever they'd play locally, the Legion Hall would be sold right out, and everybody would ask David to play one of his original tunes. He developed more and more confidence in his own material, and he started sneaking his songs into his regular act.

The big break came when David Boire and the Mustangs played a concert in Red Deer. They were the opening act, and the headliner was none other than Stompin' Tom Connors. Stompin' Tom took one listen to David Boire singing "Country Girl," and the next thing you knew David had a recording contract with

Boot Records. "Country Girl" was released as a single. The Mustangs recorded an album to follow up, and they started to play bigger bars and taverns. "Country Girl" went to number one in Australia—who knew they listened to country music way down there?—and David Boire was suddenly the biggest news to ever come out of Fort Vermilion. Even though his family lived across the river, we were all pleased to claim him for our own. He had a good run, although he did burn his way through three or four wives. But then things changed. Technology. In the early 1980s, surgical techniques had improved to the point where it seemed worthwhile for the doctors to take another look at David Boire's eyes.

David had an operation in Calgary, and they managed to restore the sight in his left eye. The other eye was a write-off, but David could see again; he could read a newspaper and drive a car and watch television. It was a minor miracle that happened there. For some reason, though, he stopped writing songs. Once he got his eyesight back, he never did any more composing. He still played in bars and lounges in Edmonton and Regina and anyplace they appreciated a good country song. He became a solo act, just him and his guitar, and he didn't do any of his own material, although I went to see him play at the lounge in the Kingsway Motor Inn in 1988, and when I shouted out a request for "Country Girl" he seemed pleased. He didn't quite remember the whole song, but he faked his way through it real nice, and he was kind enough to join me for a drink after his set. He's still out there, still playing, and at least he got to touch the elephant, even if he never got to ride it.

David Boire may have been the most famous musician to come out of Fort Vermilion, but he wasn't the best. Not by any means. The best musician to come out of Fort Vermilion was Bud Peyen, and there is nobody who would argue that point.

Bud was also self-taught, but there didn't seem to be any instrument he couldn't pick up and figure out, and his voice had at least a three-octave range. Bud Peyen could growl deep and low like Johnny Cash or float up high and light like Roy Orbison. He won the talent show every year he entered, although he was always decent enough to give away the trophy to the person he felt came in second. Winning the talent show also got you a fifty-dollar prize, and Bud Peyen did keep that cheque. He wasn't stupid. He didn't write any original songs, but he could change the lyrics around on any song you wanted to hear, always to humorous effect, and he knew so many songs he was like a human jukebox.

Bud could also draw. After my mother gave him a set of pastels and watercolours, he started to paint as well, and he would occasionally come over to our house for a visit and give my mother a drawing or a painting he thought she might like. Once he brought over his guitar and tried to teach me a few chords, but it was instantly apparent that I had no musical abilities. Bud agreed to sing us some songs instead. He did a version of Hank Snow's "I'm Moving On," changing all the words around to be funny.

Well, that big black Indian going down the track
He's got sixteen bannocks in a gunnysack
He's moving on (he's moving on)
He'll soon be gone (he'll soon be gone)
I told him twice to get rid of his lice
And he's moving on

We laughed and shouted and encouraged him to continue. So he kept playing and making up more words, and we kept laughing until my mother could hardly stand up.

A fellow from the city looked after my car
He grabbed hold of the spark plug wire
He's moving on (he's moving on)
He'll soon be gone (he'll soon be gone)
He turned it loose when he felt that juice
And he's moving on

And,

A guy named Hank got so darn drunk
He fell in the outhouse and man he stunk
He's moving on (he's moving on)
He'll soon be gone (he'll soon be gone)
Had to hold my nose when we burned his clothes
And he's moving on

I noticed that my mother had stopped laughing, and I figured it was because Bud Peyen had tossed my father into the song. He didn't mean anything by it, I knew; it had sort of popped out. The reference to Hank being drunk was unintentional as well. Bud Peyen had stopped asking my mother about my father, but I guess he hadn't stopped thinking about him. Anyway, Bud switched over to his own version of "I've Been Everywhere," and it was a thrill to listen to him rattle off the names of all those towns and cities.

I've been to Edmonton, Calgary, Regina is the place for me
Red Deer, Deer Lake, for Pete's sake
Medicine Hat, Sibbald Flats, what do you think about that
I've been everywhere, man, I've been everywhere
I've breathed the mountain air, man, I've crossed the deserts
     bare, man
Travelled, I've done my share, man, I've been everywhere

Of course, Bud Peyen had never been to any of those places, but he could sure sing about them good.

Bud Peyen went through the windshield of his truck. It happened on the road leading out of Assumption, as he was following Father Litzler. They'd both been doing some work at the Elleski Shrine, and Father Litzler ran his car into a moose. The priest had purchased a used Sunbeam coupe in Westlock or Barrhead or some other crazy place, and despite the road conditions he had decided to bring it north and restore it. He drove it way too fast, and he was always having to take the damn thing apart and fix it again, but that seemed to be part of his enjoyment. After he met the moose, the car was unfixable.

Father Litzler was just coming around the hairpin corner that lets you out of Child's Lake back onto the road to Fort Vermilion when a moose ran out in front of him. He couldn't do anything but duck, and I guess pray. His car was built low; it took the legs right off the moose, and the moose took the top right off the car. It was a horrible-looking accident, and Bud Peyen was so shocked he kept going straight instead of turning; he went off the road and nosed down into a culvert. The sudden stop sent him through the windshield of his truck and out onto the hood.

Father Litzler sat up, took a second to notice he was alive and unhurt, and went to find where Bud Peyen had parked his truck. The moose was dying, but it was obviously in pain, and he wanted Bud to get his rifle and put the animal out of its misery. The priest stumbled around looking for Bud and his truck and his rifle until he noticed the trail into the culvert. Bud Peyen looked much worse than the moose did.

It's a good thing Father Litzler did so much physical work, because he had to be strong to do what needed doing. He got Bud Peyen off the hood of his truck and stretched him out in the back, where he covered him with a blanket. He tried to stop the bleeding;

there was a lot of blood coming out of the big man. Then he used a jack to lift the front of the truck, then he used the winch Bud had on his front bumper to pull the truck out of the ditch, and then he used the sleeve of his shirt to clean some of the broken glass off the seat, and he drove that truck like a sonovabitch to St. Theresa's Hospital. The whole process, start to finish, took almost three hours, and there wasn't another car on the road the entire time.

Bud woke up at the hospital. He spotted Dr. Usman working on him. "Don't worry, Doc," Bud Peyen said, "we'll tell everybody you *shot* the moose." Then he passed out again.

We went to visit Bud Peyen in the hospital, and he was a frightful sight. His face had been cut so badly we wouldn't have recognized him, if it weren't for the size of the man. He'd broken his sternum and most of his ribs; his mouth was twisted sideways and stitched like a medicine bundle. He was alive, though, and everybody in town thought that was a pretty good deal. Bud was a tough guy; it would take more than going through a windshield to kill him. Father Litzler was considered a hero, not that he needed the praise, since his standing in the community was already so high. The priest he didn't have a mark on him, and the only damage he suffered was caused by Investors Group, his insurance company. They refused to pay the claim. They said hitting a moose was "an act of God."

We didn't recognize Bud Peyen when he got out of the hospital. Not just because he'd lost so much weight, either. I don't know if was the blunt force of the head injury or the loss of blood or the time it took to get him medical attention, but he was never the same after that accident. He had brain damage. He had trouble keeping his balance. He got migraine headaches that he took to treating with alcohol, since it was the only thing that worked. After disapproving so strongly of Frank Jones and his new tavern, Bud would go on to become one of Frank's best customers. He had difficulty carrying on the most basic conversation. He forgot how to paint, and he stopped playing the guitar. He couldn't remember any songs.

Bud had difficulty remembering people as well. I used to help him back to his house in the woods sometimes, when he was too confused to find his way home. Sometimes we'd make it all the way there and he'd have no idea who I was. That would leave me with a sad, chalky feeling in the pit of my stomach. Other times his eyes would light up with recognition, and his hideous face would break into a smile.

"Hey, little partner, how you doing?"

"I'm good, Bud. Just a little bit farther, Bud."

"How's your dad, him?"

"He's good, Bud. Just a couple more steps, Bud."

"I ever tell you about the time him and me went prospecting up north?"

"Yeah, Bud, I've heard those stories."

"You know? Your dad is the smartest man I ever met, me."

"Yeah, well, I'll tell him you said that if I ever see him again."

"Tell him I'll come up for a visit soon. I'll bring my guitar, eh?'

"Yeah, you do that. Goodnight, Bud."

To be honest, Bud could be a great big pain in the ass, especially when he started going on and on about stuff I already knew. Or when he talked about my father as if he was still living with us when he was God knows where and we hadn't heard from him in years. I was mostly grown up by this point, and I had better things to do with my time than drag the world's tallest Indian through the bush. Bud was a third the size he used to be, but he was still heavy enough.

My last winter in Fort Vermilion was the last time I saw Bud Peyen. Lloyd Loonskin and I were at the back of the Legion Hall, smoking cigarettes and flirting with girls and generally being loud and annoying. The talent show was on, and we were part of the merciless audience that would decide who would go home with the grand prize. The usual performers had come and gone, and it was widely accepted that Edward Carrier would take first place that year. Which meant I would get at least a week's respite from having to go knuckle-to-knuckle with his son Ted; Ted's father would be in a good mood for a few days and wasn't likely to put hands on any of his family. Edward Carrier would get up every year at the talent show and sing the one song he knew. He would always dedicate it to his wife.

"This song is for the most beautiful woman in the world, my wife, Bertha, and I sure hope she enjoys it," he'd say. Maybe that one moment in the spotlight each year was enough for Bertha to put up with him; he was a violent man and quick to lay a licking on her and any of their children. Bertha would sit at the front of the hall, and when her husband made his introduction, her eyes would fill up with tears. Then she'd smile all the way through his version of "Blue Eyes Crying in the Rain."

Denise Banks was next onstage. She performed an original work of poetry, accompanying herself on a native drum she had inexplicably painted green. Denise Banks was a huge white woman with a large bouffant that was suspiciously orange in colour. She was married to Donald Banks, a man who hadn't had a bath since Lester B. Pearson collected his Nobel Peace Prize. For years the two of them had been the proprietors of the only restaurant in town, the Trappers' Shacks and Café, an old house with three small sheds that visitors could, hypothetically, rent for overnight accommodation. Mostly the shacks were occupied by people who lacked the wherewithal to find another place to stay. One of the long-term tenants was a skinny little man named Watchusk who had wandered down from the Territories, had a nervous breakdown, and ended up collecting welfare cheques in

Fort Vermilion. Denise Banks collected the cheques on his behalf, since she provided his room and board. Watchusk didn't speak any recognizable language, and parents cautioned their children not to go near him. He bathed less often than Donald Banks did, and he smelled like an abandoned outhouse. In any other community he'd have been institutionalized, but in Fort Vermilion he was considered part of the local colour. Watchusk was mainly left alone, although it was fun to run up to him and ask him where his girlfriend was, which sent him into fits of rage. We all knew he'd never had a girlfriend in his life.

Lloyd Loonskin had invented that game. If it sounds cruel, well, Lloyd only started taunting Watchusk the year his grandmother died and he was well and truly orphaned. Lloyd was twelve years old when she died, we both were, and I was trying to convince my mother to let him come and live with us when the problem was solved. Gene Rogers, of all people, decided to take Lloyd in and let him stay at the teacherage, and everybody agreed that was mighty Christian of him.

Denise Banks finished her spoken word presentation, although we didn't know enough to call it that in those days, and Corporal Ledinski, the master of ceremonies, came out to introduce the next act. He had a funny look on his face, and everybody stopped gossiping and listened.

"I'm pleased to announce our final act for the evening. This gentleman hasn't been here for a while, but we're sure glad to have him back. Let's give him a nice welcome, everybody. Here comes Bud Peyen."

The place went up like a rocket. We jumped to our feet, and people were screaming and shouting and stomping their boots and whistling. Out Bud came, and he was still a big shambling mess of a man. He hadn't performed at a talent show since he went through the windshield of his truck, but here he was, carrying his guitar, and for a moment it looked as if anything was possible. Bud nodded shyly at the crowd, sat down on the stool that Corporal Ledinski had brought out for him, and started to play. Nobody said anything. Nobody moved. Nobody could breathe.

Bud Peyen slowly and painfully picked out the only song he could remember how to play. A couple of times he looked as if he wasn't going to finish, but then he'd give a little shudder and keep on going. His voice was weak and shaky, and you could hear the words getting caught in his throat. It was probably the first song he had ever learned.

> *The bear went over the mountain*
> *The bear went over the mountain*
> *The bear went over the mountain*
> *To see what he could see*
> *And what did that bear see?*
> *And what did that bear see?*
> *The bear went over the mountain*
> *To see what he could see*

As many times as I remember bad things about Fort Vermilion, as often as I think about what a hard place it could be, I remember that the people who lived there were sometimes capable of incredible kindness. There wasn't a sound in the Legion Hall until after Bud Peyen finished, and then we were all on our feet again. Bud Peyen won first place at the talent show, and that time he took the trophy home with him. He needed help getting back to his place, because of how excited he was. It seemed like a small thing to do, and I was proud of him and proud of the town and proud that I was still his little partner. He was surrounded by people; they were wishing him well, pounding him on the back and pouring out praise. All the attention made Bud tired and confused. I took him by the arm, and he looked down at me and put his arms around me. He was smiling to beat the band. He smiled all the way back to his house.

"Almost there, Bud."

"That's good, eh?"

"You did good tonight, Bud. I'm proud of you."

"Thanks, Hank, that means the world to me."

"Bud, it's not Hank, it's me. My dad isn't here, remember?"

"Hank, you remember that time we went prospecting in the North?"

"It's not Hank, Bud, it's me."

"Remember when we had that scrap with them city boys?"

"Here's your place. Watch your head, Bud."

"You know, Hank, that was the best time I ever had."

"Go to bed, Bud. I'll see you later."

"Hank?"

"Yes, Bud?"

"You know, you're the smartest fellow I ever met."

"Thanks, Bud, that means a lot."

"And Hank?"

"What is it, Bud?'

"We're friends, eh, me and you?"

"Sure."

Bud Peyen died the next winter. He got confused and couldn't remember where he lived. He sat down in a snowbank to figure it out and froze to death. There wasn't anybody to walk him home.

ten

OVING PICTURES

" **I** *don't know what to say."*

Fighting words. Not quite up there with "Just watch me" or "You shall go no farther," but fighting words nonetheless. Those words were the direct cause of the Great Fort Vermilion Movie Theatre Riot, an event that lives on in the memories of participants to the point of legend.

Fort Vermilion may not have had a television signal or a radio station to listen to on a consistent basis. We may not have had a sewer system, and most of us lived in houses without electricity, let alone running water, but we did have something that made us the envy of neighbouring communities. We had something that filled the citizens of Buffalo Head Prairie, La Crete, Tallcree and Rocky Lane with jealousy. An attraction that brought them out of their own homes and across badly maintained gravel and dirt roads into the heart of Fort Vermilion. They came from far and wide every weekend, from Assumption, Meander River, Paddle Prairie and Indian Cabins, and it was a source of considerable local pride that we had something they didn't. We had a movie theatre.

Now, this wasn't the kind of movie theatre you might find in other small towns. There was no lobby, no popcorn machine and no soda fountain. The washrooms were located out back. The seats were wooden benches. The floor was dirt, with rough planks on top. The Fort Vermilion Movie Theatre was housed in a metal Quonset hut the government of Alberta had constructed or slapped up or thrown together as a temporary storage shed for road-building equipment. The road never got built, and the equipment was finally taken away to some other northern community where it wouldn't be used. Not building things was one of the biggest employment programs in the North; many people were seasonally employed to not build roads, not build hospitals and not build schools. Workers would drift from town to town, like nomads, depending on which MLA was pushing through which pet project in the legislature.

Fort Vermilion was in what was referred to as an "improvement district," which meant, theoretically, that lots of taxpayers' money was available to improve the district. The government down south would make a decision, and the next thing you knew, some duly elected representative would show up to make a stirring speech about how this bridge, library or health centre would greatly improve everybody's life and make that particular town or district or reserve truly the Gateway to the North. This was a much sought-after designation, and half the communities that fell above the fifty-first parallel were aggressive in claiming it as their own. You can't drive more than a few hours north of Edmonton without running into several Gateways to the North. The towns of Peace River and Grimshaw, which are separated by a fifteen-minute drive, had a longstanding feud over the title, which was finally resolved when Grimshaw changed its designation to Gateway to Peace River on all the appropriate signage. Their original choice, Gateway to the Gateway of the North, was determined to be too confusing. Besides, it looked like a typographical error.

Most of the big capital projects were ignored or underfunded once the initial announcement had been made. Sometimes—and this is purely anecdotal; I certainly wouldn't want to malign the reputations of any of the fine elected officials of that era—the big project was revealed to have come about as a result of cronyism or influence-peddling. The North·is full of projects that were started with great fanfare, shoddily and slowly developed, and never finished. Bridges were built to places where there were no roads, and roads were built where there were no people. Projects would peter out as funding became more and more scarce. Sometimes they were killed outright, when the government of the day decided it was time to give the province's taxpayers a break. Since most of the paying taxpayers lived down south, abandoning a project in a remote community was always deemed the most fiscally sound way to proceed. That's how it goes. Stop construction on a half-built senior citizens' complex in Calgary, and you might run into opposition. Taxpaying people, voters even, might complain. Do the same thing in a small northern village, and nobody says a word. And if they did, who would listen?

The upside to this system was that when the big projects were abandoned, stuff was sometimes left behind. The summer of 1975 was as good an example as any. In an attempt to support Fort Vermilion's non-existent tourism industry, a wooden boardwalk was being built along the riverbank. It was three-quarters finished when the plug was pulled. Somebody must have noticed that there were no tourists in town. Anyway, the construction workers had barely downed tools when the looting of the boardwalk began. Lloyd Loonskin and I went down to collect some wood— we had plans to build a tree house or a fort—but we were too late to pick up what we wanted. The workers had been given notice at 4:00 PM, and they'd gone to pack up. By 4:15, the word had gotten out. By 4:30, the deconstruction was well under way.

The riverbank swarmed with families. Hammers and saws flew as the men ripped the boardwalk to pieces. Women and children scrambled up and down the embankment, transporting the detritus to waiting pickup trucks and wagons. The foreman of the construction crew, a large blond man with a perfect set of teeth who hailed from somewhere near Ponoka, came out on the street at about the same time Lloyd Loonskin and I arrived on the scene.

"Hey, partner," Lloyd Loonskin said, "look at that guy."

I turned around to take in the foreman. He was standing there mouth agape, eyes blinking furiously. I turned back to Lloyd Loonskin. "What about him?"

"That guy?" Lloyd Loonskin said. "He looks like he's gonna cry." Lloyd was smiling when he said it.

The rest of the construction crew slowly fanned out on the street behind their foreman. They didn't say a word. None of them even appeared to be breathing. The foreman ran one sun-burned hand across his mouth, then he gave a little shrug, almost a shiver.

"Jeez," he said. "Jeez, you guys." He didn't seem to be talking to anyone in particular. "You could have at least waited until we left town."

Lloyd Loonskin gave him a benevolent smile. "Mister," he said, "if everybody waited, then all the good stuff would already be gone." Lloyd turned and gave me a look, as if to say, "See, I told you we should have got here earlier."

The Indians had fallen on that boardwalk as if it were a dying buffalo. They were devouring it, taking everything apart. And just like in a buffalo hunt, nothing went to waste, and nothing would be left behind. Glenn Lambert was building himself a work shed. He had plenty of lumber already, so he concentrated on the hardware. By some sort of unspoken agreement, he got first choice of any nail, screw or bolt. Ted Carrier wanted to put a proper floor on his mother's house, so he went mainly after the prefinished waterproof slats along the railing. Bud Peyen staggered up the hill carrying an impossibly heavy load of pressure-treated posts. He gave me a grin as he passed by.

"Hey, little buddy, look at this. I got enough firewood for all winter." He continued on past the foreman and his crew, stopping to give them a polite nod of appreciation. Even after his accident, he was still relentlessly polite. "That's real good wood, fellas," he said. "Gonna burn nice and slow."

It must have looked fearful to those construction workers. It must have been a terrifying thing to see. The entire two and three-quarters miles of completed boardwalk was gone before the sun went down. The crew boarded their bus and crept out of town. The boardwalk was doomed from the start, anyway; it would have been wiped out in the first high water of the spring.

The Quonset hut that housed the Fort Vermilion Movie Theatre was also recycled. At one time the government had planned to build the Red Earth Road, a shortcut to Fort Vermilion from Edmonton that would have saved three or four hours. A winter-only forestry road already existed, but it was in such poor repair that no one would travel on it unless they were fleeing from the law or something of that significance. The paving for the Red Earth Road had started simultaneously at the north and south ends, the idea being to meet in the middle, but the money ran out after only ten miles or so on each side had been completed. To this day, they haven't finished putting down the asphalt. People travelling to the North for the first time will often look at their road maps and decide to go up the Red Earth Road to save a little time. Don't make this mistake yourself. Before the work on the Red Earth Road started, however, the road crew had erected a Quonset hut in Fort Vermilion to store their graders and earth-movers and other equipment. One year later all of that equipment was gone, and we had ourselves a movie theatre.

Ellen McAteer was the visionary who saw potential in the abandoned garage. She was a widow lady. Not a grass widow like so many of the women in town. Ellen McAteer's husband was actually dead. He had accepted a position with the school division but died shortly after arriving in Fort Vermilion. Ellen McAteer took to her bed for several months. Since she and her husband had been new in town, nobody bothered to see how she was doing, and by the time she emerged from her period of mourning she had gone a little crazy. The town decided she was, in the words of Bud Peyen, "bug-jack wackadoo." Not that anybody held this against her. The town was full of people who would, in other communities, have been institutionalized. One more nut wasn't going to ruin anything.

Ellen McAteer got herself a job working at the post office. It kept her busy. That was a good thing, since she was a busybody. She wasn't an ugly woman by birth, but as she got older she became more and more nasty in appearance. Her face was composed entirely of sharp angles. Her eyes were watery and distrustful. Her skin was pallid and her hair colourless. She was the whitest white woman anybody had ever laid eyes on.

She terrified Bud Peyen, and on the rare occasion that he'd needed to see her in her professional capacity, he had always asked my father to come along for moral support.

"That woman scares me, Hank," Bud would say. "She's so damn pale."

Ellen McAteer was indeed a formidable presence. She served on every committee in town, and she never missed a meeting.

She had deeply held religious beliefs, but had never managed to become friends with Father Litzler. He tolerated her as member of his congregation, but it was apparent that he couldn't stand her.

The Fort Vermilion Movie Theatre was, literally, the only show in town. After the road crew departed, Ellen McAteer purchased the abandoned equipment shed, hung a huge chunk of canvas across the back wall, and hired a couple of Mennonite boys to build seats and a projection booth. She didn't bother putting up a sign out front, or giving the town's first movie theatre a proper name. She simply called it the Fort Vermilion Movie Theatre. The rest of us called it "No Refunds."

Ellen McAteer would never give your money back, for any reason. Once the money went into the cash box, it stayed in the cash box. It didn't matter if the movie print was scratched, or if the movie shown was not the one promised, or if the reels got mixed up and shown in the wrong order, which was a fairly common occurrence. Any complaint, any request for reimbursement, any suggestion that you were owed something was met with a terse "No refunds." And that was that. You paid your money and you took your chances.

Ellen McAteer showed films on Friday and Saturday nights. The season was mainly spring and summer, since the building wasn't insulated and the only heat came from a wood stove at the back. Showtime was seven in the evening, unless people were late arriving; then the movie might start as late as eight or nine. It cost one dollar for adults and fifty cents for children. Stale bags of potato chips and room-temperature bottles of grape pop were available for a less than reasonable two bits. There were no tickets. You simply waited until Ellen McAteer opened the doors and rushed inside to choose your seat. Grownups sat near the back and kids down near the front.

Just before starting the movie, Ellen McAteer would go up and down the aisles with her green metal cash box collecting admission. It was like church. If you timed it right, you could move up after she collected from the bench in front of you and avoid paying altogether. Ellen McAteer had to be momentarily distracted for this to work, and Lloyd Loonskin and I would take turns causing a mild disturbance. This was risky, however. If you got caught, you'd be banned from coming back for some appropriate amount of time. Worse, you'd be given a severe dressing-down that would delay the start of the movie and get you punched in the stomach by the other kids.

Once the money was safely in the cash box, Ellen McAteer would go up into her booth and start the film. She owned a single 16-mm projector, and between reels she would turn on the lights, rewind the reel you'd watched, thread the next reel into the projector, and then turn off the lights again. This would take ten to fifteen minutes, unless some kid slowed things down by buying some chips, definitely a stomach-punching offence. On average, it took three hours to see a feature. It's not like there was anything else to do. Besides, every time the lights came up, you could look around to see if anybody had changed seats or been caught kissing. Adults would visit, catch up on the news; it was a fairly sociable way to spend the evening. Smoking wasn't permitted while the movie was running, but grownups lit up in between acts, resulting in nicely diffused images by the time the show concluded.

The Fort Vermilion Movie Theatre was a gold mine for Ellen McAteer. Almost two hundred people could squeeze into the Quonset hut, and the place was usually filled to capacity for both the Friday and the Saturday shows. There was almost no overhead. No advertising was required. The metal cases carrying that week's film would come by truck from the bus depot in High Level and be dropped off at Stephen's General Store every

Wednesday. By Thursday, the whole town would know what was playing on the weekend. Always careful to present entertainment with a good moral message, and mindful of the tastes of her audience, Ellen McAteer programmed a steady diet of cowboy movies and Elvis Presley musicals. Once she brought in an Elvis movie that was also a Western, and the demand was so great she had to add on extra screenings. None of the films she showed were first-run features. Many of them were in black and white, and the quality of the viewing experience was low. But it didn't matter. We had a movie theatre.

I can still remember the thrill of it all. The lights would go down, and we'd be somewhere else. Someplace better. Good guys and bad guys and action and excitement. We'd travel to places that none of us, not one of us, could ever hope to really see.

Even at fifty cents a ticket, the moving pictures were a luxury. We didn't get to go every weekend, and our mother could rarely afford to send my brothers and sisters and me as a group. We did, however, come up with a reasonable solution. Jobs were scarce enough for adults in Fort Vermilion, and there were even fewer ways for a kid to make money. If stealing wasn't an option, you were limited to hunting for beer bottles to redeem at Stephen's General Store. It wasn't the fastest way to make a buck. But if we combined our resources, we could usually raise enough cash to send one of us to the show. That person would then be responsible for filling everyone else in on what they'd missed.

We started off taking turns. My brother Dan had a fantastic memory, and he could describe the plots of movies in great detail. My brother Sean was the designated viewer for musicals, since he could not only tell us what had happened but be counted on to deliver perfect a cappella renditions of most of the songs. My talent lay in embellishment. I would come home and act out the entire movie, playing all of the characters, adding and deleting scenes or changing endings, always with an eye to making the movie as exciting as possible. Lloyd Loonskin was the first to pick up on this.

"Hey, partner, I seen that movie with you, and I don't remember Audie Murphy shooting two guys with one bullet."

"Yeah, but wouldn't it have been cool if he did?"

Word spread, and I would spend the week after seeing a show performing it for larger and larger audiences. I never outdrew Ellen McAteer, but my popularity got a boost. Lloyd Loonskin received a regular allowance from Gene Rogers now, but he stopped going to the movies every weekend. He would send me in his place every time I couldn't afford a ticket.

"I'd rather watch your movie than the one playing at the theatre," he said.

If I had known what Lloyd Loonskin went to the movies to escape, I like to believe I wouldn't have accepted his generosity.

It wasn't that difficult to improve on the movies Ellen McAteer showed at her theatre. Hoot Gibson seemed old-fashioned even to us. Elvis Presley was fine, although I wanted him to do more punching and less singing. My most interesting challenge was overcoming Ellen McAteer's censorship. Every Thursday afternoon, she would privately screen whatever movie had been dropped off, looking for profanity or lewd conduct. At the weekend shows, she would turn off the sound to blank out swearing, forcing us to lip-read desperately. During interactions that were the least bit sexual, she'd put her hand over the lens of the projector, leaving us to puzzle things out from the soundtrack.

My re-enactments left out nothing, another reason for their popularity. As it turns out, my versions were much racier than the content being censored. When I finally got around to renting *Nevada Trail* a few years ago, I was surprised to discover the love scene was extremely chaste. Not to brag or anything, but my version was an improvement.

God forbid we should see Elvis Presley kiss Ann-Margret, but we could watch John Wayne shoot a thousand Indians. We watched so many Indians get killed on screen it became annoying. I routinely changed the endings of the movies I'd seen, killing off all the cowboys when I acted them out. Then Ellen McAteer made the mistake of showing *Billy Jack*. Any aboriginal person over the age of thirty-five can tell you where they saw this movie *and* quote it from memory. It was the first movie any of us had ever watched with an Indian as the hero. Not the bad guy. Not the sidekick. The hero. Sure, Tom Laughlin didn't look like a real Indian, but neither did those Italian or Jewish actors we were used to seeing play aboriginals. *Billy Jack* was the all-time number-one box-office draw in Fort Vermilion. It played for six weekends in a row. Then Elvis returned. This time, however, nobody wanted to see him. The Duke followed. Same thing. People stayed away from the theatre. For the first time ever, it wasn't operating at capacity. Ellen McAteer was stunned. She sought help from a higher power.

"I don't know, Ellen. It's not my, uh, my problem," said Father Litzler. He went back to work on his beloved tractor.

"Yes, I can see how it would be a concern," said Constable Ledinski. "But I'm not sure what you want me to do about it."

"Maybe you should show *Billy Jack* again," I said. I was being sarcastic.

"Yeah," said Lloyd Loonskin, "bring back *Billy Jack*." He was completely serious.

Having apparently exhausted the advice available from the town's leading citizens, Ellen McAteer had cornered two of her best customers outside the post office to ask us our opinion.

"That's ridiculous," she said. "I can't keep showing the same movie over and over again."

"Why not?" Lloyd Loonskin asked.

"People will get bored and stop coming to my theatre."

"They're not coming now," I said.

"What did you say?"

"Nothing," I said.

"Indians!" That was Lloyd Loonskin, who sounded genuinely enthused. Mrs. McAteer turned her head to look at him. There weren't any flies on her, that's for sure. You could tell right away she knew what he was getting at.

"That's why everybody came to see *Billy Jack,*" Lloyd said, getting more and more excited. "Because he was an Indian, and he could beat everybody up, and he wasn't scared of anybody." He smiled his lopsided smile at Ellen McAteer. "I bet if you showed another movie about Indians, everybody would turn up to see that."

Ellen McAteer put the word out that she was ordering in a special movie just for the Indians. And the half-breeds and the Metis. This time she even ran a few posters off on the Gestetner machine at St. Theresa's Hospital. The wording was simple; the posters simply said that she was proud to be presenting (or pleased to announce, I don't recall which) an all-Indian action film at the theatre on the upcoming weekend. People were dubious about whether there was such a film, but as the week wore on excitement started building, and Ellen McAteer drew a sold-out crowd for the Friday showing. The film was called *Red Gorge,* which was close enough to "redskin" to make everybody think that, if it wasn't exactly an all-Indian film, there was at least a strong possibility of some action, "gorge" being close enough to "gore." Lloyd Loonskin was convinced it was a film about Chief Dan George.

About half of the town had turned out for the movie. It took Ellen McAteer twice as long as usual to work her way through the crowd to collect her money. The lights went out. The title

Red Gorge came up on the screen, which elicited a cheer from the crowd. The reels were in the right order. The cheer died down as the titles kept running. There was something terribly wrong. The actors' names were written in some foreign language. The first scene had an elephant in it, ridden by a man with a beard and a funny wraparound hat. The elephant entered a courtyard, and there was another man waiting there. He was wearing an orange jumpsuit and standing by a fountain. The man looked right at the camera, right at us, then said something in a language none of us could understand. The bottom of the screen lit up with English subtitles. What the man in the orange jumpsuit had stated, apparently, was, "I don't know what to say." The bearded man on the top of the elephant replied, "You resemble a spider," possibly losing a little something in the translation. Then both men started to sing.

We were stunned into silence until the dancers came on screen and everybody figured out what was going on. The dancers were wearing saris. Just like Elisabeth Usman, Dr. Usman's wife. Elisabeth Usman was a large, jolly Danish woman adored by all. She had shocked most everybody when she wore her wedding sari to her first big do in town, but people got over it. This was different. Not only were people getting a musical when they'd been promised an action film, they were angry that Ellen McAteer, after living in Fort Vermilion for so long, couldn't tell the difference between a real Indian and someone from India.

It started fast. The first song wasn't even over when someone began stomping on the floor. Everyone else joined in. It wasn't loud, the way 200 people would sound stomping on linoleum or tile, but it was loud enough to make Ellen McAteer turn up the volume on the movie. Next, everybody started whistling. All at the same time, and all through their teeth. Then someone—I know for a fact that it was Lloyd Loonskin—started the chant.

"We want our money back, we want our money back, we want our money back."

Ellen McAteer turned the picture off, turned on the lights, and told everyone to go home.

"I'm going to call the police," she said. That was an empty threat, since "the police" consisted solely of Corporal Ledinski, and he was in the theatre watching the movie. He apparently had been hoping for a good Indian action film, too, because he stood up and faced her. Everybody stopped making noise.

"I'm right here, Ellen," Corporal Ledinski said, "and I want my money back, too."

Nobody cheered. Nobody applauded. We were too overwhelmed. We had won. The Great Fort Vermilion Movie Theatre Riot had succeeded. We had done the impossible. We got refunds.

Lloyd Loonskin walked me back to my house, making sure I got there in one piece. Ted Carrier was awfully good at holding grudges.

"Why so glum, chum?" I said.

He didn't say anything back. I pressed on.

"You look down," I said.

"What do you mean?"

"We have won a great victory today over the forces of darkness," I said. "You should be happy."

"Sure."

That was it. We walked in silence the rest of the way to my house. As he was leaving, Lloyd Loonskin put his hand on my shoulder and looked at me directly.

"You ever think," he said, "if we all got together, you know, like at that boardwalk, or like tonight at the movies, but we did it about something important . . . "

He trailed off, and I wasn't smart enough to know where he was going.

"Yeah?"

"Well, maybe, don't you think . . . if we all got together about something important, couldn't we do something?" He smiled, but even I was perceptive enough to notice it was a sad smile. I decided to lighten the mood.

"What do you mean 'we,' white boy?" I said. I waited for Lloyd Loonskin to laugh, but he didn't.

"That's right," he said. "You're not a real Indian."

I swear it looked for a moment as if he'd gone funny around the eyes. But it was probably the way the moonlight was bouncing around that night. We shook hands, and I went inside to perform my version of the all-Indian, all-action, non-stop-excitement movie *Red Gore* for my brothers and sisters.

eleven

LAZY GUY

here were more and more white people in Fort Vermilion. It seemed as if a new crop of folks from out was arriving every year. It got so you could walk around and hardly see anybody you knew. New houses were being built and more power lines were going up, and it was all happening because someone had figured out there was oil and natural gas in the North. That meant money and jobs, although neither of them seemed to be going to the Indians. Everything was speeding up, too, and that made some of the locals nervous. I thought it was fantastic. As far as I was concerned, they could tear the whole town down and build something new to replace it.

Lloyd Loonskin and I were hanging out in front of the Sheridan Lawrence Motor Hotel. It was an impressive-looking structure, two storeys high and made out of cinder blocks. The men working on it had all been brought up from Edmonton, and they were housed in Atco trailers. If you looked into the enormous picture windows at the front of the hotel, you could watch the work being done on the tavern.

"It's going to be the largest beer parlour north of Peace River," I said.

"I guess so," said Lloyd Loonskin. "Takes up half the building."

"Frank Jones is a smart guy," I said.

"Frank Jones," Lloyd Loonskin said, "is a weasel."

It may have seemed as if we were watching the construction, but really we were just wasting time. We were both thirteen, turning fourteen in a few months. We were teenagers, which meant we wasted most of our time.

A small restaurant was also being installed in the hotel, and we figured this addition had something to do with Alberta Liquor Control Board regulations, since Frank Jones didn't seem to be putting much money or effort into it. At the back of the building were twenty hotel rooms, on two floors, with an indoor corridor running down the centre. Each unit had its own private bathroom with hot and cold running water, a queen-sized bed and a television set. The televisions were causing people to shake their heads. The only person in town who owned one was Scott Wagner, the manager of the Hudson's Bay store, and even with the fifty-foot antenna he had installed he could pick up a snowy picture only if the weather was good. But Frank Jones hadn't lost his mind. He knew that the government of Canada was tossing Anik satellites up into the sky and that we were going to get a signal sooner or later. Besides, he got a good deal on the sets.

Almost everyone in town was excited about the Sheridan Lawrence Motor Hotel. The grownups couldn't wait for the beer hall to open up, and many people were looking forward to the new restaurant. Both the food and the service at the Trappers' Shacks and Café left a lot to be desired, and everybody still told the story of the prim and proper new schoolteacher who had stopped at the café for a meal. Her cheeseburger ended up with one of Donald Banks's Band-Aids in it; Donald wasn't very handy with a knife, or any sharp-edged object, and he was always cutting himself and bleeding all over the kitchen. The bad part was that this lady had finished half of her cheeseburger before the Band-Aid made itself known. She'd tried to get Dr. Usman to pump out her stomach, but the doctor wouldn't bite.

"Look at that monkey." This was Lloyd Loonskin, and he seemed in a really grumpy mood.

"Which monkey would that be?"

"That guy over there. All he's doing is lifting stuff and carrying stuff."

The guy in question did look a bit like a monkey, the way he used his arms and moved around the job site.

"Well, what about him?"

"Shit, I could do that."

"Me, too. What's your point?"

"That guy? He's probably making ten bucks an hour."

"That doesn't seem right, does it, boys?"

This was a stranger talking. He had come up behind us and joined our conversation. He startled us both, but Lloyd Loonskin held his ground. I jumped a foot in the air.

"A project like this should be a boon to the local economy."

Lloyd and I didn't know what to say. The man standing behind us had light brown hair, almost blond, and the bluest of blue eyes. His hair was long and braided, and he was wearing a fringed buckskin jacket. It was everything we could do not to burst out laughing. He was the funniest-looking *mooneyow* we'd ever seen.

"It's time for a change, and that's why I'm here," the man said.

"Excuse me, mister?" said Lloyd Loonskin. "What's that?"

"I'm here to start up an employment equity program. A new government initiative," the man explained.

Neither of us had a clue what he was talking about, but the word "government" was enough to make Lloyd and me suspicious. It was like Bud Peyen always said: the biggest lie you'll ever hear is "I'm from the government and I'm here to help you."

"Nice talking to you," said Lloyd Loonskin.

"See you," I said.

"Wait," the man said, talking directly to Lloyd Loonskin. "A project like ours can help a young fellow like you become employable."

"Yeah?" said Lloyd Loonskin. "What about him?" He jerked his thumb in my direction.

"Well," the man said, "this project is specifically targeted at members of the First Nations."

Neither of us had heard that expression. We stared at him blankly.

"It's an aboriginal employment program," the man said.

"Ohhhh," I said.

"Jobs for Indians," Lloyd Loonskin said.

"Yes," the man said. "The goal is full employment for all our peoples."

He actually did say peoples. And he put some spin on the word, as if it meant something important.

Lloyd Loonskin couldn't resist the opening. "What do you mean 'our' peoples, white man?"

I missed the expression on the man's face, because I was too busy falling down laughing, but Lloyd Loonskin told me later that the government man's face turned so red he almost did look like an Indian.

With everybody else in town, we soon learned that the man's name was Andy Maracle, and he was a Mohawk from the Six

Nations reserve in southern Ontario. That was so far away it was incomprehensible. Andy Maracle was in Fort Vermilion to start up a pilot project aimed at furthering employment or reducing the welfare rolls, whichever came first, and he wasn't having an easy time of it. The Indians in town kept making him pull out his treaty card to prove he had full status, and even then they didn't believe him. They thought he dressed weird, too.

The idea behind the Aboriginal Initiative Opportunity, and that's what the pilot project was called, was to break the cycle of dependence. (No, really, that's what it said in the brochure.) There were a distressingly high number of families relying on welfare in Fort Vermilion. The fur trade was almost non-existent, and the lumberyard had been gone for years. Any job that did spring up like a flower in June was given to an outsider. Did the government decide to deal with any of these issues? No, what they came up with was the Aboriginal Opportunity Initiative, which meant that no able-bodied Indian male would be allowed to collect a welfare cheque. Instead, people would be paid the same amount of money every month to go around Fort Vermilion *doing* stuff. Like fixing the swing set in the schoolyard. Or picking up trash from the side of the road. Or doing good deeds.

Andy Maracle had almost got it right. The Aboriginal Initiative Opportunity wasn't a boon to the local economy, but it was a boondoggle. It was a make-work project. And it pissed off people on welfare who would have gladly taken real jobs. They responded, as Indians often do when faced with official stupidity, by defaulting to their passive-aggressive worst—or best, depending on your politics. The Indians made Andy Maracle repeat his instructions over and over again, as if they were hard of hearing or unable to understand simple commands. They did their assigned tasks as slowly as possible. Some even went as far as being rude, which was unusual, but Andy Maracle had earned their distrust early on. He annoyed everyone by giving last names like Lambert and Courterier their French pronunciation. And he'd held a sweetgrass purification ceremony on the first day of the project. The Bush Cree and Beaver Indians didn't know from sweetgrass. It was like offering communion to workers on a kibbutz.

The intransigence of the local aboriginal population may have been frustrating to Andy Maracle, but he had it coming. If he'd asked around, he would have found out there wasn't a single man in town who didn't want to work for a living. Except one.

Tommy Francis was, hands down, the laziest man on earth. If there had been a world championship for laziness, he'd have been—well, he probably wouldn't have shown up, so who knows what he would have done. His laziness was much remarked upon in Fort Vermilion, but not in a pejorative manner. We were all impressed with Tommy's total lack of initiative; it was as if he was allergic to work. It was breathtaking to see somebody that bone-lazy, and it made him a celebrity.

Not a celebrity the way David Boire was. But Tommy Francis was in the same category as Warren Mitchell, who was the best runner. Warren would win the foot races at the summer sports day every year, and Corporal Ledinski had once timed him with a stopwatch and claimed afterwards that he'd run a four-minute mile. In his cowboy boots. So Warren Mitchell was the fastest man in town, and Donald Banks was the dirtiest man, and Tommy Francis was the laziest man. These were all character qualities to be admired.

Tommy Francis lived common-law with Hannah Lizotte (no relation to Narcisse), who had adapted quickly to Tommy's preferred lifestyle. They both ended up being enormously fat, although Hannah Lizotte had an excuse because she turned out children on an annual basis. Bud Peyen had once told my father that it was easier for Hannah and Tommy to have a new kid than to keep the old ones clean, and he may not have intended it as a joke.

The entire family lived in the new housing development. It was informally called "Chicago Town," after *Sheekug,* the Cree word for skunk, because the septic field had been improperly designed.

Lloyd Loonskin had lived next door to Tommy Francis and Hannah Lizotte and their family, and he didn't miss his old neighbours at all. Hannah Lizotte would shout the same thing to her children every morning when they left the house.

"Where you going?" she'd yell as her kids darted into the bush.

"Out," they would shout back, more or less in unison.

"Well," Hannah would say, before waddling off into her kitchen, "make damn sure you come back."

Lloyd Loonskin could have cheerfully killed the entire family.

"Every day it was the same thing, eh?" he told me.

"Sounds annoying."

"It was almost like they didn't know any other words."

Tommy Francis wasn't prepared to give up his life of leisure for any Aboriginal Opportunity Initiative. He liked not working. He liked collecting a welfare cheque every month. He liked receiving the baby bonus. He liked sleeping in late and drinking beer and doing as little as possible. He had completely converted Hannah Lizotte; she liked all the same things. Except she also liked playing bingo.

Tommy was so late on his first morning as a member of Aboriginal Opportunity Initiative that Andy Maracle gave him a warning.

"I'm putting a letter of reprimand in your file, Mr. Francis."

The next day Tommy didn't show up until after lunch.

"This is your second warning, Mr. Francis."

Tommy didn't show up at all on his third day with the program, and that earned him an angry visit from the initiative's leader.

"I'm going to be crystal-clear about my expectations, Mr. Francis. You either show up, on time, and fully participate, or you will be removed from the program."

"I'd get fired?" The hopeful tone in Tommy Francis's voice further irritated Andy Maracle.

"You would be removed from the program and lose your eligibility for government assistance. It's not like being fired from a job, Mr. Francis."

Tommy Francis shrugged. He'd never had a job, so he had no idea what being fired from one was like. The shrug sent Andy Maracle over the edge.

"It's people like you, Mr. Francis, who give the rest of the aboriginal community a bad name. Are you going to feel proud the next time someone calls a member of the native community a lazy Indian? Are you?"

Tommy Francis *was* actually proud of being a lazy Indian, and he didn't see why this would make Andy Maracle upset. It was none of Andy Maracle's business, really, plus he kept shouting, which was making Tommy Francis jumpy. He was about good and ready to get up from his couch and—nah, too much trouble.

"I don't understand you. There's no reason you should be behaving this way. It's not as if you're disabled."

The word caught Tommy Francis's ear, and he stood up so fast he frightened his wife and children.

"Andy," Tommy Francis said, "you've done your job. I'll be there tomorrow morning bright and early."

And so he was. He showed up on time and in his uniform of blue coveralls and yellow hard hat. The members of the Aboriginal Opportunity Initiative were cutting down brush at the riverbank that morning. Tommy Francis, whistling cheerfully, picked up an axe, went to a stump, removed his work boot, and cut his big toe off.

"You did that on purpose," said Andy Maracle. He was driving Tommy Francis to the hospital, and the words came out as a snarl.

"Nah," said Tommy Francis, "it was an accident."

The problem was, Tommy Francis hadn't taken into account the fact that a retired microsurgeon from Bombay, reduced now to doing basic medical procedures, might welcome a challenge.

"Don't worry, Tommy," Dr. Usman said. "I managed to save your toe."

He said this to Tommy in his hospital bed, after he came out of the anaesthetic. Tommy was crushed. His plan was ruined because Dr. Usman had decided to get creative. Not that Tommy didn't enjoy his few days of bed rest at St. Theresa's, but there had to be something he could do to make things go his way. He decided to get his toe infected. Once he was home he didn't follow the instructions Dr. Usman had given him, and he didn't change the dressing on his toe once. He ended up back in the operating room. When he regained consciousness, he saw that Dr. Usman had a serious look on his face.

"Tommy, I managed to save your toe," he said. "Again."

Tommy Francis started to cry. Dr. Usman may have thought they were tears of joy, but Tommy was weeping in frustration.

"Don't worry," Dr. Usman said, "you've only lost a bit of mobility. The toe still works fine." And, to add insult to injury: "I think I did some of my best work on you."

Great, Tommy Francis thought to himself. On *my* pitch he decides to hit it out of the park.

Tommy was back at work three weeks later. After a day on the job, he dropped a length of sewer pipe on his foot, crushing that same big toe. The toe was so badly damaged that Dr. Usman had to amputate it. In the course of things, blood tests and x-rays and whatnot, it was discovered that Tommy Francis had an irregular heartbeat. He could have left his toe alone. He actually *was* disabled, just enough to get out of participating in the Aboriginal Opportunity Initiative.

"I never thought being lazy would be such hard work," Tommy Francis said.

Andy Maracle wasn't happy.

"Can you hurry up with them forms?" said Tommy Francis. "I want to get them in the mail today. The sooner I send them out, the sooner those disability cheques will start rolling in."

The story of Tommy Francis and his big toe was all over town, but Lloyd Loonskin filled me in on the details he'd picked up from being part of the same crew. My mother worked next door to Dr. Usman at the hospital, so I had some inside information to share with Lloyd as well. Andy Maracle fled Fort Vermilion, and the government shut down the Aboriginal Opportunity Initiative. It wasn't because of anything Tommy Francis did, but because someone, somewhere, realized the program was a stupid idea. Nobody missed it when it was gone.

"I hated working there," Lloyd Loonskin said.

"You mean you hated *not* working there," I said. "Tommy Francis may be allergic to work, but none of the rest of you were breaking a sweat too often."

"Exactly," said Lloyd Loonskin. "It was like we were practising how not to work hard, and we were starting to get pretty good at it, too." He shook his head. "I was starting to feel like a lazy guy."

The government wouldn't leave us alone, though. The next thing we knew, our MLA was coming to pay us a visit for the very first time. Lewis "Chunky" McNabb had been a popular disc jockey at CKYL Radio, the voice of Peace River. He had been elected to the legislature as part of Peter Lougheed's sweep to power, and he was going to be at the Legion Hall to make a big announcement. There'd been some rumours about it, and almost everybody thought this was going to be trouble. Lloyd Loonskin and I thought it should be good for a laugh, so we decided to attend the meeting.

Here's what Lewis McNabb had to tell us. The government of Alberta, in partnership with Ottawa, was going to spend $7 million to build a bridge across the Peace River. The ferryboat I'd managed to destroy before I was born had been replaced by one powered by a tugboat. And now the end of the ferry was at hand. Lewis McNabb was obviously expecting an enthusiastic response from the crowd, but nobody seemed pleased at his announcement, and there were two guys at the back of the room who kept interrupting his speech and asking him questions. Annoying and ungrateful questions: where would the bridge be located and how had that decision been made and would there be jobs for the local people, and if so, what kinds of jobs would they be? The one man was tall and rangy, with impressively nicotine-stained fingers. The other man was short and square-shouldered, and almost completely bald. Both men sported the kind of sunburn you get from a lifetime of working outside. Both were wearing faded blue jeans and flannel work shirts, and the taller one had on a leather bomber jacket. Farmers, maybe, or trappers, but they were definitely getting on Lewis McNabb's nerves. He decided to put them in their place, and he filled the hall with the rich tones of his professional broadcaster voice.

"Gentlemen," said Lewis McNabb, "I would love to stand here and answer your questions all day, but you don't seem satisfied with the answers I'm providing, and there are other people in this room who may want to hear what I have to say."

"If you would *give* us any answers, we might find them satisfactory." That was the short, bald man.

"You haven't said one thing that makes sense." That was the tall drink of water.

"Well, since you seem determined to monopolize this meeting, I have a question for you," Lewis McNabb said huffily. "What is your standing in this community?"

"I'm the peace officer," said Corporal Ledinski.

"And I'm the parish priest," said Father Litzler.

I don't want you to think the Indians were sitting back quietly and letting someone else do their fighting for them. They weren't. They just didn't know what to do. One of the obvious sites for the bridge was on sacred land. The land was so sacred and so holy that they weren't allowed to talk about it to anyone from outside, and that included the government. Father Litzler and Corporal Ledinski were concerned about local jobs, and they had taken an instant dislike to the new MLA. But they didn't know about this sacred land, either.

And now Frank Jones was standing up to say something.

"Most of you know I own that plot of land upriver," said Frank Jones, "near Rocky Lane."

There was murmured assent. One hundred per cent of them knew that.

"Well, that's got some people worried, because they think maybe that's where this new bridge might go," he continued.

His comment made many of the people in the room angry, because it sounded as if Frank Jones knew about the sacred land. That wasn't right, since he had been raised Christian, not Traditional. Somebody must have spilled the beans.

Everyone in the room was scowling and nodding, and not in a nice way, either.

"Well," said Frank Jones, "that's not going to happen."

Lewis McNabb dropped his pencil.

"My good friend Lewis McNabb here and I certainly discussed that possibility, but I've decided it's important to leave that property alone. The bridge will go somewhere else, and I think that's a fine thing."

Frank Jones sat back down. It was a toss-up as to who looked more shocked by his announcement, the people in the room or Lewis McNabb. Frank Jones would have made a killing selling that land to the government, and it was not in his nature to pass up an opportunity to make a buck. What happened? Money happened, is what. It wasn't until six months later, when the location of the bridge was officially announced, that it all became clear. Frank Jones had sold the section with the sacred land to his good friend Warren Pritchard. That's because he'd already learned the government was going to build the bridge a hundred yards west of the ferry landing, nowhere close to there.

The project meant more workers showing up from the city. Three young men who came north to be part of the survey team got a little drunk one day and picked up a local girl and got her drunk and gave her some marijuana and then took her out of town for a bush party. They were polite about it, though; they drove her back to town when they were finished with her.

The news flashed through the moccasin telegraph, and Father Litzler heard enough to suggest to Corporal Ledinski that they go over to see if the girl would press charges against the survey workers. Her mother wouldn't let the Mountie or the priest into the house. She sent them away. She told them nothing had happened. She told them to mind their own business. The next night someone kicked in the door of the Atco trailer those three boys were living in and beat those boys half to death.

Corporal Ledinski investigated the assault. It was obvious who was responsible, but there were a hundred witnesses who said that the girl and her mother and her father and her uncle had been at a Tea Dance on the night in question, and it had lasted all night long, like a good Tea Dance should. Even though there hadn't been a proper Tea Dance in town for many years, that was the story people stuck to. No charges were laid. The family left town and never came back.

The more white people came, the more Indians left. Looking for work, mainly, or better prospects. Father Litzler died, and he was buried at the Elleski Shrine. The next day the Indians built a Spirit House over his grave. Fabian Noskiye packed up his family and moved them away. His granddaughter was Lucy Noskiye. She was the girl taken out into the bushes by those surveyors. His grandfather was Augustus Noskiye, the last of the Medicine Men. I went to see Augustus the month I turned fourteen. It wasn't my idea. Lloyd Loonskin made me do it.

"You should take him a present, you," Lloyd Loonskin said. "He saved your life, and now you're a man and you should thank him properly."

"I may not be a kid any more, but I'm not a man," I said.

"Man enough," said Lloyd Loonskin. "Take him some tobacco."

Augustus Noskiye and his wife, Sophie, seemed glad to see me when I stopped by for a visit. We sat down at the kitchen table.

"Elder," I said, "I brought you a present."

"Thank you," he said. "You're a good boy." Augustus Noskiye rolled a cigarette. "There's too many white people around here these days."

"There sure are," I said. Then, catching his expression, "You can't mean me." I was trying to make a joke. "You made me an Indian."

"Maybe." He started chuckling. "We'll see."

For some reason I felt sad, and the harder he laughed the sadder I got. It was the strangest damn thing.

"You know what?" the old Medicine Man said. "With this new bridge everybody will be able to find us now. More white people are going to come in and try and help us. You know what? It was better before. When they didn't know we were here. When they left us alone."

"But things are easier now," I said. "It's progress."

I wasn't thinking only about the bridge. I was thinking about indoor toilets and electricity and television and all the other improvements that had happened in Fort Vermilion since I was a little boy.

The Medicine Man closed his eyes. He looked as if he was going to sleep.

"We can't keep living in the past," I said.

Augustus Noskiye opened his eyes and slowly got to his feet.

"I think maybe you shouldn't come back here to visit again," he said.

He said it so kindly I felt like bursting into tears.

"Just because something is easier," he said, and he was already closing the door on me, "doesn't mean it's better."

That winter, Sophie Noskiye passed away in her sleep, and Augustus decided to go with her. They had been married for seventy-six years. He lay down next to her and turned his face to the wall and made himself die. He was the last Medicine Man.

twelve

LONG **GONE**

It was the longest trip you could ever take. It wasn't the distance, although it was pretty far, but it was the time it took and what that time took from you. The journey was made easier if you had good company. Someone you liked. I had Lloyd Loonskin. He was going along with me as far as Peace River.

It was the end of my last summer in Fort Vermilion. I was fifteen years old, and I had convinced my mother to let me go to high school in the city. My brother Dan had already left home. He'd spent a winter with Canada World Youth, travelling through Mexico, before moving to Calgary to go to college. We'd all missed him when he first went away.

Getting to Edmonton meant taking the bus. You could drive over to the airport in High Level and catch a plane, but the only people who could afford to do that were government workers. Everybody else got on an old school bus in front of the new new gas station, which had replaced the old new gas station, which had burned down. The school bus was painted white and green. It didn't have air-conditioning or proper heating or a washroom in the back. It made one trip a day to High Level. It left Fort Vermilion at nine in the morning, and if you were fortunate you made it to the Greyhound bus terminal in High Level in the nick of time for the noon bus to Peace River. The next part of the trip took eight hours, with stops in every town along the way. Then you waited at the Peace River depot until the bus from Edmonton showed up. It didn't leave until 10:30 PM. The last part of the trip took four hours, getting you into the city at almost three in the morning. Total distance travelled: 526 miles. Time spent in transit? Almost eighteen hours.

Lloyd Loonskin and I hadn't seen much of each other that summer. He'd spent it hauling supplies in and out of the bush for forest fire crews, which paid considerably more than my job, pulling weeds at the Experimental Farm. I'd saved $846, which was enough to get me heading south. Lloyd had saved enough money to move out of the teacherage he'd shared with Gene Rogers. Denise Banks had shut down the café part of the Trappers' Shacks and Café, but she still had three cottages for rent. Lloyd was living in one of those.

The previous summer, Lloyd and I had spent a month together in a tent in a campground in southern Manitoba. My mother had sent Dan, Sean and me down to spend some time with my father. He had somehow ended up in Brandon, teaching at the university there. I'd asked my mom if Lloyd could come along, too.

"Hey, partner, remember when we went camping with your dad that time?"

"Of course I do." How could I not remember? Lloyd hadn't stopped talking about the trip since we got back. He was getting as bad as Bud Peyen.

"He didn't know I was coming, eh?"

"No, he knew. You weren't a surprise or anything. It's not like my mom didn't tell him."

"Yeah, he was sure owly then, him."

There were only a handful of other passengers on the bus, which meant we'd been able to get seats at the front, the least bumpiest place. The dust was making us cough, and we had to shout over the noise of the engine.

"He wasn't mad at you, Lloyd. He was mad because my mother didn't stick around and wait for him."

My mother had dropped the four of us off in Edmonton, in front of the MacDonald Hotel. She was driving on to British Columbia with the girls and Billy to see her family. Billy had wanted to stay with the boys, but my mother wouldn't let him. I'd teased him relentlessly about it, and he had lunged over the front seat to attack me.

"How come your mom didn't wait for your dad?"

"I don't think she wanted to see him," I said. "Or maybe she knew he wasn't going to be on time."

My father had been an hour and a half late picking us up. Even though he knew Lloyd Loonskin was coming with us, he had acted surprised to see him. My brother Dan had acted as if he wasn't happy to see my father. There was much tossing of suitcases and slamming of car doors before we got on the road to Brandon.

"I didn't think we'd be camping out, me."

"Me, neither, Lloyd. I thought we'd stay in an apartment."

Whenever I tell people that my father put the four of us in a tent in the middle of Brandon's Curran Park for a month, leaving us to fend for ourselves, they react with astonishment and disapproval. It's not as if he totally abandoned us, though; he stopped by every weekend to drop off food and money.

"That was sure a good time, that one," Lloyd Loonskin said.

"It was the best time," I said. The bus was reaching the outskirts of High Level, and I had started to feel nervous.

"We sure had us some fun," Lloyd Loonskin said.

We did at that. There was a creek running through the campground, so we went swimming every day and cooked hot dogs
over an open fire, and I figured out how to get free pop from the
machine beside the concession stand.

There were also girls to chase after, or at least for Lloyd Loonskin and me. Sean was a little too young, and Dan had spent most
of the month throwing a hatchet into a tree. When my father
dropped by on weekends, he brought along a younger woman he
introduced as our cousin. That didn't fool us for a second, but it
bothered Dan some that our father had a girlfriend.

"Hey, Lloyd, remember that girl with all the freckles?"

"The one that taught you how to French kiss?"

"That's the one, and don't get cheeky. She kissed you as well."

"It wasn't my first time," said Lloyd Loonskin.

"Weyeh."

The girl was the daughter of a dentist from Winnipeg. Her
family had been at the campground for only one weekend, but
she'd managed to kiss both Lloyd Loonskin and me on separate
occasions. It was my first kiss, and I can still remember everything about her.

"What was her name, again?"

"Her name was Trudy," I said.

"That's right."

"She sure surprised me. It felt kind of gross at first," I said.

Lloyd Loonskin arched one eyebrow. This expression was
something new, and he'd been practising it for months. It didn't
have quite the effect he wanted, though. It made him look as if he
had to pee.

"It didn't feel gross to me," he said. "It felt perfect."

"Big shot," I said.

"Like how it's supposed to be."

Lloyd Loonskin seemed about to say something else when the
Fort Vermilion bus lurched to a stop. We climbed down, knocked

as much of the road dust off each other as we could, and climbed on board the Greyhound for Peace River. This time we sat at the very back, across the aisle from the washroom.

"This is a nice bus," Lloyd Loonskin said.

"Compared to what?"

"The Fort bus."

"Well, it's better than that."

"Anything's better than that," Lloyd Loonskin said.

The Peace River bus pulled out of the gravel parking lot and onto the highway. I was excited. It had taken me three tries to get my duffle bag properly stored in the overhead bin.

"Hey, partner, did I ever tell you about that fire?"

"Which one?"

Fighting forest fires was one of the most desirable jobs in Fort Vermilion. The hours were long, the work was dangerous, but the money was good. Fire crews lived in the bush the whole summer long and got their pay all at once at the end of the season. You could always tell when the forest fire season had ended. The Indian kids got new bicycles.

"The one up in the Caribou Mountains."

"That was a big one," I said. "We could see the smoke in town."

"That's the one."

"What about it?"

"Sixtoes Mitchell started that fire."

"You're lying," I said.

The fur trapping industry had dried up by then, and Sixtoes Mitchell fought forest fires as a way to supplement his income. He was a Push with his own crew, and they were considered to be the best fire team in Alberta.

"Why would Sixtoes Mitchell start a fire?"

"So he could put it out," said Lloyd Loonskin. "He said he needed the money."

That made sense. Preventing fires didn't pay as well as fighting fires.

"You gave your mom half your summer money, right?"

"That's right." I had actually given her three hundred dollars, but I figured that was close enough.

"But you're okay for money?"

"I'm good," I said. "Remember what my father always used to say: 'If you're in an interesting place, and you've got fifty dollars in your pocket'"—Lloyd jumped in to join me on the last part—"'you rule the world.'"

That's how we passed the time. Two good friends, best friends, shooting the breeze and reminiscing. Lloyd Loonskin was mainly interested in talking about the past, and we kept talking all the way to Keg River Cabins, where the driver took a break and we got out to stretch our legs. It was good to get some fresh air. People were smoking on the bus, and the air inside was thick and blue.

"What are you going to do when you get to Edmonton?"

"Well, let's see. I'll find a place to live and get some kind of weekend job, I guess."

"What school are you going to?"

"Don't know yet," I said. "I'm going to look up the biggest school in the city and go to that one."

"Yeah," he said, "probably schools down there with a couple of hundred students."

"Lloyd, there are schools down there with a thousand students."

"That's something, eh?"

"More people than in our whole town."

"Hard to imagine."

"My brother lives in an apartment in Calgary, and there're twelve hundred people in his building."

"Hey, partner, remember that time . . . "

And we were back to talking about the past again. That carried us through almost the rest of our trip. The sun dipped below the tree line, tossing long shadows across the highway. We continued our conversation, but the cool blue nightfall made us talk in whispers.

Talking about school got us remembering our break-in attempt. When I told Lloyd how pissed off I was that he'd got away scot-free, he surprised me by revealing that the nice young schoolteacher who caught us had given him the strap. She had hit him, once on each hand, lightly, then burst into tears and run out of the room.

"Hey," Lloyd Loonskin said, "you ever get the strap from Gene Rogers?"

"Oh, come on," I said. It was odd for Lloyd to ask a question he already knew the answer to.

"On the rear?" he said. "Or only on the hand?"

"On the hand," I said. "Three hits on each hand, just like you, just like everybody else."

"Never on the rear?"

"Nah."

We were tired by now, yawning, and we fell silent until we got to the hill leading down into Peace River.

"We're here," said Lloyd Loonskin.

"Yeah," I said. "I can see the Kentucky Fried Chicken guy." The Bruin Inn had been torn down and replaced by a KFC franchise years before. The tower with the revolving bucket on top was the first sign of civilization you saw as you headed south.

We dragged my duffle bag outside and left it stacked with the other luggage waiting for the bus south. Down the hill a bit we found a Chinese restaurant about to close, and we grabbed a meal there. After that, we strolled around a bit, looking at the sights.

"This place is ever big."

"Not as big as Edmonton," I said.

"Big enough," he said.

"Bigger than Fort Vermilion," I said.

"It's big in Fort Vermilion sometimes," Lloyd Loonskin said. "It's small and big at the same time."

It was dark on the street. I couldn't see Lloyd's face, but his voice sounded like a stranger's. We started back up the hill.

"You're being brave," said Lloyd Loonskin. "You're not scared?"

I was terrified. But staying behind, not ever getting out, frightened me even more.

"No," I said. "Not really."

"Remember that time we went camping together?"

"Yeah," I said.

"That was a good time," Lloyd Loonskin said.

"You'll come down," I said. "Even if only for a visit."

"I doubt it," he said. "I don't think I'd like living away from home."

For some reason, that made me angry.

"Come with me," I said. "Right now. Climb on the bus."

"You're lucky," he said. "You can just leave."

"So can you," I said. "What's this lucky crap?"

"You were born lucky," Lloyd Loonskin said. "Not me. I was maybe lucky to be born."

I put my arm around his shoulder. "Come to Edmonton," I said. "We'll get a place together, find jobs, chase girls, have some fun."

"No," he said. "This is as far as I go."

We turned past the buzzing Rexall Drugs sign. We were almost at the bus depot.

"When Gene Rogers gave me the strap, he always hit me on the rear," Lloyd Loonskin said. "He never did that to you, huh?"

I shook my head.

"You know, he'd make you bend over and put your nose on the desk. Then he'd put one hand on your back to hold you down and then whale away."

"Yeah, I heard he did that," I said.

"Sometimes he'd make you take your pants down and strap you on the bare behind."

I didn't say anything.

"Sometimes his hand would move," said Lloyd Loonskin. "Kind of wander. And sometimes he'd shove his thumb up your ass, you know."

My ears were making this rushing sound, and it was hard to think of anything to say.

"But that never happened to you?"

"No," I said, "it never did."

"You were lucky."

"I guess so," I said.

"Hey," Lloyd Loonskin said, "that's my bus there. People are already getting on."

It was the same bus we'd ridden down on, now gassed up and cleaned up and ready to head back north. I walked Lloyd Loonskin over.

"You'll come home soon," he said. "I'll see you then."

"I don't think so," I said. "You'll have to come down and visit me."

Lloyd got on and the door swung shut and the brakes hissed and the bus slowly pulled out. Lloyd Loonskin was sitting up front, by the driver. I waved at him, but he didn't see me. The big dummy was looking out the wrong side of the bus.

"There he goes," I said.

The air felt cold, and I gave a little shudder. I went into the depot and bought myself a cup of hot chocolate from a vending machine. Then the cold was gone and I was too hot, as if I had a fever. I was thinking about what my best friend had told me.

I stared at my reflection in the window of the bus station. Stared through myself and out into the night. I should have told Lloyd that I would miss him, that he was my sidekick, that he always would be. I didn't tell him that Gene Rogers *had* tried to give me the strap on the rear after my father left town. When he pulled down my pants, I pulled them back up and turned around and yelled at him not to touch me or I would tell my mother and she would tell my father and my father would come back to Fort Vermilion and he'd have to answer to him. I could have said, "It wasn't only you. There's nothing special about you, Lloyd. He's evil, that's all. Gene Rogers is evil, and that's all there is to it." That would have been a good thing to tell Lloyd Loonskin.

I was falling asleep on a bench by the time the bus arrived. It had started to rain, so I got my jacket out of my duffle bag and put it on. There was an envelope in one of the pockets. When I pulled it out, I saw that Lloyd Loonskin had written my name on it. His handwriting was precise and neat; when they taught us the Palmer method at school, he had practised and practised. Inside the envelope was a fifty-dollar bill. I had never seen one. Written on the back of the bill was "Good luck, partner!" and "I'll see you soon."

"No, you won't," I thought. "I'm never coming back and I shall never see you again."

I got on the bus. It pulled out of the parking lot and turned left at the statue of Twelve Foot Davis, then started its groaning journey up the hill. I was long gone, heading to the city, and I was so awake it felt as if I would never have to sleep again. The hum of the engine and the slapping of the windshield wipers were one big sound as we rolled out onto the highway, heading south.

epilogue

did see Lloyd Loonskin one more time. It was a big year for me. I was turning thirty. My first play had been produced, and my second one was in rehearsals. I had, surprisingly, fallen in love for the first time in my life. I had partnered up with a friend to run a new comedy club, and I was starting to become world-famous all over Edmonton. Best of all, I hadn't had a drink in almost a year.

The comedy club would fail. The friendship would crash and burn along with it. That would give me permission to fall off the wagon, and I would fall so hard I'd end up in the hospital. Of course, I didn't know any of this at the time.

I was inside the club, getting ready for the first performance of a new improv show, when I heard a ruckus in the lobby. The box office girl came rushing in to find me. She was, as always, dressed in black from head to toe. Her hair was dyed black, her fingernails were painted black, and all this blackness must have affected her disposition, because she had a gloomy personality.

"Sunny," I said, because that was her name, "what's going on?"

"There's a drunk Indian in the lobby, and he wants to come inside."

"Oh, well," I said. "Nobody loves a drunken Indian."

She didn't get it. She stared at me vacantly until I sighed and went out into the lobby.

"Hey, partner, long time no see."

Christ on a Popsicle stick. There he was, live and in person. Lloyd Loonskin. He didn't look that drunk, but man, did he look old. He could have passed for fifty, even though we were the exact same age, give or take a day.

"Lloyd," I said, "is that you?"

"Don't you recognize me?"

"Yeah, of course. What are you doing here?"

"Came to see you," he said. He made a sweeping arm gesture to include the lobby. "Came to see your show."

"Great," I said. "Let's talk outside."

We went and stood on the sidewalk. It was cold out there. Lloyd was telling me that he had hitchhiked down from Jean D'Or Prairie, where he was living, and decided to look me up. I could see his breath while he talked.

"How'd you find me?" I said.

He gave me a grin and pulled a small book out of his jacket. It was a child's diary, but there wasn't any writing in it. Just some newspaper articles glued to the page.

"See, partner," Lloyd Loonskin said as we paged through the book, "this is a review of that show you did in Calgary, and this is from that theatre magazine . . . "

"Where'd you get these?"

"Your mom, she sent them to me," he said. "I asked her."

The most recent article had been in the newspaper the day before. He had already glued it into his scrapbook.

"That's how I knew where to find you," he said.

We talked a little longer, and then I said I had to get back to work. I lied and told him the show was sold out. It was opening night, and I had enough things to worry about.

"Some other time," I said.

"Sure," he said. "Next time."

I gave him some money, forced him to take it. We shook hands. Lloyd Loonskin was halfway down the block when he turned around and came running back, holding up the handful of bills I had given him.

"Hey, partner—"

"You keep it, Lloyd. You keep that money."

"No, I wanted to say something."

"What?"

"I don't blame you."

I didn't bother asking him what he meant. There were so many choices.

I forgot about Lloyd Loonskin for a couple of days. I was reading the Saturday paper, hoping to find a review of my new show, when I spotted the story about him. There weren't many details provided. Aboriginal, blah, blah, blah, intoxicated, blah, blah, blah, exposure. The newspaper didn't say Lloyd Loonskin was once a boy who'd had a whole town looking for him and celebrating his return. They spelled his name wrong. They got his age wrong, too. He was only twenty-nine.

Whoever wrote that story about Lloyd Loonskin missed the most important part.

Sometimes it just runs in the family.

Lloyd Loonskin was lucky to be born.

I was born lucky.

author's note

Most of the characters in this book are based on
real people. Some names have been changed
for artistic reasons. Other name changes were
made for reasons of confidentiality. Some characters have also
been combined. For example, the Hudson's Bay Company sent a
new store manager up to Fort Vermilion every couple of years. I
can barely keep their names straight myself, and I see no reason
why the reader should make the effort. Some events have been
compressed, and dialogue has been invented.

It is important to point out that Gene Rogers is a fictitious
character and not a depiction of any real person. More abuse was
perpetrated than can be ascribed to any one person. Because of
his attitude and behaviour towards Indians, the character's name
was created by combining the names of two famous big-screen
cowboys, Gene Autry and Roy Rogers.

acknowledgements

I *have many people to thank,* beginning with Joanna Kotsopoulos, Kelly Mitchell and the other fine folks at Douglas & McIntyre, especially tiny perfect publisher™ Scott McIntyre, who believed in this book when it was just a conversation. Barbara Pulling is the finest editor in the world. I was lucky to get her, and her contribution to this manuscript was invaluable. I appreciate the advice I have received from the redoubtable Carolyn Swayze, who is a most excellent literary agent. Thanks also to Carl David at the Royal Equestrian in Los Angeles for providing me with a place to write, and to Max Fett at Hi-Tech computers in Burbank for the laptop.

My brother Will Ferguson read an early version of this book and was generous with his advice and criticism, as was my brother Sean Ferguson, and I can't thank either of them enough. My other brothers and sisters will recognize bits and pieces of themselves in here, and I want to thank Vivian Carter, Margaret Ferguson, Dan Ferguson, Lorna Robson and Darla Ferguson for putting up with me for so long. Thanks to David Boire for allowing me to quote from his song "Country Girl," and thanks also to the rest of the sidekicks: Wendell Lambert, Carl Mudryk, Yves Faucher, Kevin Ehman and Jeff Haslam. Sorry I wasn't a better friend. Carol Greyeyes, Bill Brumbalow and Carl Hare have my gratitude for being such good teachers. Most of all, I want to thank Antoine Courterier for saving my life.

about the author

Ian Ferguson is an award-winning play-wright (*Elephant Shoes, Uncle Joe Again, Naming the Animals, Bone Crack* and *The Daughters of Judy LaMarsh,* among others) and humorist. He has written extensively for television and radio, and he is the creator of the live improvised soap operas *Die-Nasty* and *Sin City* and the creator and co-executive producer of the CBC comedy show *Liquid Soapȝ.* He is currently developing a series for American television.

With his brother Will, Ian Ferguson is co-author of the runaway best-seller *How to Be a Canadian,* which was shortlisted for the Stephen Leacock Medal for Humour and won the CBA Libris Award for best non-fiction book of 2002. He lives in Los Angeles with his spouse, Kirsten Van Ritzen, and their dog, Lucy.